Body Blows

Other books by Tim Miller:
Shirts & Skin

Body Blows

Six Performances

Tim Miller

with a foreword by
Tony Kushner

photographs by
Dona Ann McAdams

The University of Wisconsin Press

The University of Wisconsin Press
1930 Monroe Street
Madison, Wisconsin 53711

3 Henrietta Street
London WC2E 8LU, England

Printed in the United States of America

ISBN 0-7394-2599-4

For my partner Alistair McCartney
My love for you is beyond boundaries

Contents

Foreword

As a tribute to Tim, I'm typing this naked.

No, really, I am. I have never typed naked before. It would no more occur to me to type naked, in the ordinary course of things, than to eat dinner naked, which I have also never done and probably never will. My mother would not have approved, to put it mildly. I grew up in Louisiana, and Tim grew up in California, and that's probably the difference, nudity being a West Coast kind of thing, or so it always seemed to me. In Louisiana we had too many mosquitoes. But thanks to Tim, here I am typing naked. I am missing my clothes. I am wishing I was twenty-one. Or thirty-one, even. I am noticing ways in which I am forty-five. It's interesting, typing naked. I am trying not to look down at my . . . hoo-hah, as we used to say in Louisiana.

Read Tim Miller and you think about your body. Tim performs so many functions for his community: artist, hero, griot, goad, gadfly, crush material. One of these functions, somewhere in between artist and hero and goad, is his serving to remind those of us who need reminding that the movement that has transformed

our lives—let's call it the sexual minoritarian liberation movement—
is an affair of naked bodies, the bodies of others and Others and of
one's own body as well. Tim reminds us that liberation means
trying something new. Well, he doesn't just remind us: he shocks
and exhorts and teases and dares us, he invites/seduces/entices us
to renew our understanding of liberation as a politics of eros,
cathexis, astonishment, as a willingness to try something new, to
make and to be made new. For so many of us sexual minoritari-
ans, for so many of us Americans (all of us heirs to and indebted
to various revolutions in the name of freedom) liberation has
become a depressingly over-rehearsed, routinized consumption
of ossified fetishes, rainbow necklaces, internet porn; and then
there are those of us who claim the road to liberation wends a
backwards way through membership in the GOP, or through
the commodification and marketing of "post-liberation" self-as-
contrarian-libertarian internet columnist. For all of us, Tim
Miller's many functions are aspects of one absolutely necessary
function: artist/articulator of the two inescapable truths of revolution, of liberation: be brave enough to move forward, and know
where you've come from.

In this book you will meet (or renew acquaintance with) one
of the real originals, a man whose writing and performing, whose
epic, Herculean labor is shaping an antithesis to both the shrunken
selves of consumerism and the shriveled selves of creeping con-
servatism. Tim is self-declaring, self-critical, self-analytical, self-
celebrating in the full-throated Whitmanic mode, democratically,
expansively self-celebrating. Tim sings that song of the self which
interrogates, with explosive, exploding, subversive joy and freedom, the constitution and the borderlines of selfhood. He is one
of selfhood's internationalist activists. For the truly imaginative
mind, for the truly adventuresome spirit, for the truly living heart,
introspection, memory, interiority do not lead one into isolation
and implosion. Self-exploration is revealed by work like Tim's to
be only another path, perhaps the highest, truest path, to the

world at large, to other people, to the communal, the social, the political. Proust knew this, and Tim is in some ways like Proust, a compulsive converter of lived experience into art, of self into art, of memory into art; only Tim is happier and healthier and he likes people more than Proust did and Tim isn't French and Tim gets out of bed and leaves the cork-lined room.

Tim probably doesn't even have a cork-lined room. Does he actually have a fixed address? He is Johnny Appleseed, the Wandering Jew, he's not only gotten out of bed, he seems never to sleep, he's traveled all over the country and the world, he seems always to be in a new town, he must have met more gay men than Kinsey. Tim's writings—what to call them? I hate calling them "pieces," they're too complete; "plays" implies fiction, lying, so that's no good; "essays" conjures visions of tweed jackets patched at the elbows, of professional opinion-mongering mutts like, oh never mind; "monologues" is uncomfortably redolent of stand-up comedy, auditions, of monofocus, solipsism, monotony—anyway, Tim's writings form a history of what it is to be one kind of gay man, one kind of queer, one kind of sexual minoritarian in America from the days immediately preceding the advent of the plague, from the days of the plague called Reaganism through the plague years of AIDS and into the present, when both of those plagues are still with us, political and biological viruses ceaselessly mutating to evade our defenses. Tim is a veteran of both wars, the war against AIDS, the war against the Reaganite/Gingrichite/Bushist counter-revolution. He is the quintessential artist-as-activist, proof that you can do it and live to tell about it (if you're lucky). Tim has come to us, in 2001, scarred but not bowed, and his presence in this impossible time—who believed some of us would still be here?—at this impossibly advanced calendar date, Tim Miller in 2001 is, to me and I would imagine to many of us, a paradoxical figure of grieving and action, of mourning and resistance. His work promises: the viruses will be stomped. And it ceaselessly reminds/cautions: but only through our efforts.

I saw Tim's *Paint Yrself Red/Me & Mayakovsky* at PS 122 in Manhattan more than twenty years ago. I went because he looked cute on the poster and because I was so excited to find a gay man making art about Mayakovsky! I found not the revolutionary nostalgia I imagined but an amalgam of that tradition and everything that was contemporaneously cool, smart and sexy, progressive— I found Mayakovsky's animus in Manhattan, the hots I'd carried for the doomed wildman of Red October smoldered afresh. I encountered an artist capable, at his best, of eliding the ostensibly insuperable barrier separating the political and the personal, the political and the aesthetic, whirling incommensurables into a vortex from which new meaning flows. And I discovered that one could be multitudinous even when alone onstage.

So what else to say? You think you don't need to hear such singing? You think you don't need to type nude? You think Tim won't make you do it? He will! You do! You must! Read the book! Turn the page already and get started! Finish the book already and get active! Tim is here to tell us: Our work is far from finished. And our lives depend on our action, on our engagement. Here is a reasonable manual for engaging: the heart, the mind, the spirit, the body. Go forth and be like Tim.

I have to put my clothes back on. Without pants, my butt is sorer than I think it would otherwise have been from this much sitting. So I have discovered that pants apparently cushion the butt. Who knew?

Tony Kushner

Acknowledgments

Though this book now hangs out on a shelf or bedstand, it really was birthed on the stages of theaters, universities, and performance spaces all over the world. I feel lucky to have had these works nurtured by so many heroic arts organizers who gather their communities and make events happen on a dream, a song, and sometimes even *out of their own checkbooks*. Each of these venues—and there are hundreds I could mention—is gathering the artists, energies, audiences, and activists in their communities to make the fiercest culture possible. I thank them all.

I want also to thank a few of the friends, co-conspirators, and colleagues who have helped bring my performances and writing forward. I am deeply grateful to David Roman, Glen Johnson, Holly Hughes, Jeff McMahon, Annie Sprinkle, Mark Ball, Leslie Hill and Helen Paris, Mark Russell, Ken Foster, Jill Dolan, Martin Sherman, Linda Frye Burnham, Joan Hotchkis, Ian McKellen, Donald Hutera, William J. Mann, Danielle Brazell, Abe Ryebeck, David Schweizer, Robert Pela, Rhonda Blair, Mel Andringa and

John Herbert, Shannon Jackson, Sally Banes, David Eppel, Allan Gurganus, Laurie Beth Clark, Michael Peterson, Karen Finley, Howie Baggadonutz, Patrick Merla, Therese Jones, Patrick Scully, Joan Lipkin, Ed Hunt and Jeff Rodgers, Jerry La Bita, Phil Setren, Lois Keidan, Del Hamilton, Hae Kyung Lee, Bonnie Cullum, Jeanne Pearlman and Donna Garda, Ed Decker, Vicki Wolf, David Zak, James Levin, Howard Shalwitz, the UCLA School of Theater, and of course, Raphael Kadushin and everyone at the University of Wisconsin Press! Special thanks to Doug Sadownick, who shared with me many of the years when I made these performances.

I am eternally grateful to my dear friend Dona Ann McAdams and thank her for twenty years of photographic and psychic support. All the images in this volume are used with her kind permission.

Finally I thank my partner Alistair for his open heart and constant support in my work and in our life together over the years. I dedicate this book to him in gratitude for the love, grounding, and inspiration he offers me so generously.

Introduction

This book explores the tangible body blows—ones taken and ones given—of my life and times as explored through my performances. The lights come up bright on stage and we find ourselves right in the middle of some kind of queer boxing ring. The blows come fast and furious. The gay-bashers' blows. The sweet blowing breath of a lover tickling over my eyes. The blows on my shoulders and head from a cop in Houston or San Francisco during an ACT UP (AIDS Coalition to Unleash Power) protest. The stubborn butting my head against the homophobic crap that gets dumped in my path. The below-the-belt blow of HIV-AIDS that almost had us on the ropes. The exquisite, soft touch of two men's bodies coming together in loving sex. I hope my shows are full of the put-up-your-dukes and stand-your-ground feistiness of such day to day blows—given and received—that are a part of being gay in America. I raise my voice as a performer to honor these Slings and Eros of our outrageous queer fortune!

In my twenty years of work as a performer and writer I have tried to tell a few such stories that chart the emotional, spiritual, sexual, and political topography of my identity as a gay man. Okay, I admit it, all this highfalutin' stuff as well as wanting to divulge some juicy autobiographical tidbits from my love life! I have assayed this gnarly chore by whatever theatrical means necessary: garrulous ranting, bittersweet two-hanky narrative, correspondence school tap-dancing, cheerful nudity, poetic mapping, and socially transforming soap-box standing! Whatever the creative avenue, this commitment to trying to articulate a queer life has been at the center of my work as a performing artist since 1980, when I did my earliest performances in New York City at Performance Space 122 at the age of twenty-one and organized the first gay men's performance art festival in the United States.

I believe my mission as an artist and a gay man is to give witness to this challenging time, to live out loud and give that voice to my community, and to throw down a big bejeweled Liberace gauntlet to our backward society.

One of the things I think theater can do quite well is to gather communities into over-heated rooms in order to shine a light on systems of prejudice that are just so damn unfair. The sweaty reality of live performing has been a great place for me to cast my personal creative high beams on the tasty pleasures and nasty injustices that queer folk face. I feel lucky that I get to gather with people in cities all over the country to raise awareness, encourage activism, stir the dating pool, and test-drive strategies for lesbian and gay equality. The right-this-instant heat of live performing is an especially handy cattle prod to encourage people to get behind that steering wheel and hit the road. I believe the empathy and openness that come through the seductive strategies of performance—compelling narrativity, the performer's charisma (if it's a good hair day!), the group dynamic with a live audience, and so on—create the ideal lab conditions for conversion, for channeling the audience's psychic and political energies

Buddy Systems, 1985

toward claiming inner and outer transformation. I think theater is primarily a big mirror that can be held up to the community. In that reflection we can see a set of potential roadmaps to new sites where liberation stories yet-to-be-told can flourish.

The performances included in this volume explore all kinds of kiss-and-tell joys and sorrows of this gay boy's life. I hope my work creates spaces for savoring the humor and humanity of queer identity in America as well as confronting the grim, parallel reality of the array of U.S. human rights violations against lesbian and gay people. As I follow the bread crumbs trying to get out of that damn forest and away from the witch's glowing oven, is it just me or does that witch look strangely like Jesse Helms? Hmm, could just be a lighting problem.

I'm Not Alone

Though almost all of the performing I do is solo, I feel like I am never really alone on stage or in the theater. Sure, in the theoretical sense, my solo performances exist in relation to my sense of community and the times we inhabit, but this feeling of not being alone is much more human-scaled than that abstract notion. I see each individual performance's audience as my creative partners, as companions of the night's revels and co-creators of the night's revelations. My performances are a real-time encounter with the acknowledged presence of the folks seeing the show. I'm talking to them *specifically*.

The encounter starts before the show does. Audience members often get greeted by me as they arrive at the theater or performance space. I do this to reduce the performer-spectator divide, natch, but also because I just happen to like hanging out in the theater lobby before the show. Let's face it, there's always more action in the lobby than in my dressing room backstage. Plus sometimes there's no bathroom back there and you have to piss in a tennis ball can or in the vase filled with rancid water from last week's production of *Ain't Misbehavin'*. It's a glamorous life on the road! At least in the lobby I get to pee with the grownups in the clean toilets before I go onstage.

The partnering with the audience doesn't stop there, of course. Like a sweaty tent-revival preacher, I tend to press the flesh during my shows and to get pressed back—sometimes even pinched on the butt if the audience is frisky on a Saturday night in St. Louis! I hope reading the scripts of the performances will suggest the immediacy of the interactions between me and the audience. The spectators have all kinds of different relations with me. They tattoo me, scrub cake off my face, give me the Heimlich maneuver, wash my naked body, let me read their palms, pull me around by ropes, shout out "pussy" and "asshole," and eat oranges from my hand in a fruity communion. In *My Queer Body* I wander naked among the rows and finally end up sweaty on one person's lap, eye to eye as we try to find our way out of hell. The collaborative ritual of the evening is completed in my extended hangout with the audience after the show. A quick swig of water in the wings and I immediately head back to the lobby and meet, commiserate, give and receive advice, hug, sign books, and in my saucy days on the road before I was a married man, swap phone numbers! All of these exchanges are a chance to rehearse, to try out, some of the possibilities I propose in my shows.

Just as I never feel like I am alone out there on the mostly bare stage, I never feel like the performance space is empty either. Though I usually have only one or two props, this is not just me wanting to create "poor" theater in a Grotowskian sense. Sure, some of it is determined by my lean-and-mean budget constraints since I get no government funding for my performances. Anything that's going to go with me on the road has to fit in one carry-on bag with my clothes; otherwise it's too much expense or bother and isn't going to end up in the show. The truth is I prefer to allow the quicksilver imagination of the audience to work with me and make things appear and disappear with the minimum of fuss, muss, and shipping fees. My performance landscape is just me and a dangling orange on a string, a seedpod from Walt Whitman's grave, a piece of lava from a volcano, a circle of some dirt from outside the stage door, or some pasted-together maps from my old *National Geographic*s. Occasionally I need a footlocker, a stool, a milk crate, or a piece of rope, all items that can readily be found stashed somewhere in most performance spaces or theaters.

In spite of the spare formality of these spaces I create, I actually feel the lushness of the world there in the performing arena. The handful of dirt is my backyard garden, the maps become my gorgeous cosmological backdrop, the seed or orange becomes the fertile garden, the Edenic possibility that recurs again and again in my work. My stage space needs to be blank enough so it can serve as a surface on which the audience and I can imagine new social relations.

On my performance itinerary are frequent visits to authoritarian public buildings and symbols of government. A show might feature a demonstration at a county hospital, a glimpse of queer empowerment at the San Francisco City Hall, the harsh, chipped Formica corner of an INS official desk, or a future inaugural gala at the Kennedy Center in D.C. for the first black lesbian president of the United States. The wish fulfillment inherent in creatively fucking with these power-of-the-state architectures is consistent with my desire to encourage, to imagine, a kind of a psychological inner theater where we redesign more equitable social spaces for human beings to occupy. I don't want to commit energy to creating a theatrical *set* of the Supreme Court, I want the audience to help in changing the *actual* Supreme Court. My "set" or "properties" are ultimately going to need to be continually co-created by the people who see my shows once the performance is over. In a way, we all become stage hands to make this happen. Between interacting with the performer and giving their utopian thinking a workout, audiences have already had some practice imagining, rehearsing even, the potential for social, emotional, and sexual transformation. Hopefully they are also then more prepared to keep that work going a bit as they head back out into the world.

Body! Sex! Self!

Theater is a chance for people to be in a dark room with a bunch of other sweaty bodies and see what might happen. If it's a good night, they should want to get laid or storm the barricades or shout mystic visions from whatever rooftops they might have handy. One of my biggest chores is to offer a menu of a new relationship to our bodies and sexuality. Some of my strategies to make this happen are frank and poetic sex talk, images of orgies bringing down the federal government, and of course the naked body barging onto the stage.

I hope my performances offer audience members, both straight and gay, an opportunity to renegotiate their relationships to their bodies through the performer's embodiment and the slinky tales I weave. This process is nothing new. I think the theater has always been a place where the presence of the body is allowed. I'm sure those audiences in the fourth century B.C. were looking forward to checking out the fresh meat and seeing the new crop of cute chorus boys at one of Euripides' opening nights. This is probably part of the reason why nudity onstage is such a staple of edgy new performance maneuvers. In our fucked-up American culture right now, the theater is virtually the only place (other than the occasional, remote nude beach!) where the naked body is allowed a public presence in real time. The minute I take my clothes off in these performances—and I do in all of them except *Stretch Marks*—the whole theater changes. The spectators shift in their seats, stop breathing, become aware of their sweat making their underwear stick to their legs.

In my own work I am more interested in using my naked body as an avenue for exploring the most vulnerable, human, humorous, and fucked-up parts of myself than in using it as a seduction to display the cutest possible person in the cutest possible light at the cutest possible moment in the show! I hope that will mean that nudity onstage can be seen as part of the palette of things theater artists can explore in performance. A naked weenie or butt is not that interesting in itself but rather becomes important for us to look at as it reveals the feelings, complexity, desires, details, and revelations of our lives.

In a way, all of my work is about being cast naked out of paradise, the Ur-drama of Western civilization. The first performance

in this book, *Some Golden States,* takes place in that backyard garden of my childhood home in Whittier, a kind of low-rent Garden of Eden with a K-Mart nearby. The show begins with my
hometown's earthquake shaking the clothes off my body. Cast
out of "paradise" by the shaking of my world, I paper-clip a leaf
over my crotch and head almost naked into the world.

Awareness of my nakedness and the culturally communicated
shame that piggybacks on our skin is a crucial tension in all my
work. I was a big nudist as a child, always sneaking around naked
when no one was looking. Intuitively I knew that my naked body
was a kind of secret weapon, my best hope to fight back against
the cultural signals that discipline us to imagine we're somehow
dirty and unworthy. In the performance script of *My Queer Body,*
I remember . . .

> when I was a little boy. I would come home from church and
> take off all my clothes, the suit the tie and the tight shoes, and
> put my naked little boy's body between the polyester sheets.
> Loving the feelings on my skin. Making them mine. Reclaim-
> ing my body from church and state.

(The long arm of the law would catch up with that kid when
the National Endowment for the Arts would take away his grants
in 1990 for reclaiming his naked, queer body and sexuality, but
more on that in the introduction to that show.) We meet that
anarchic little boy again in *Glory Box* when I get naked in a charming section about how I used to take off all my clothes when I was
five and climb in my mom's wooden hope chest. I would snug-
gle into my mom's fake chinchilla bolero jacket to breathe in that
cedar-drenched world. My adult naked body in the performance
becomes sweetly redolent of childhood longing and memories
and invites all the metaphors that we can cram in that hope chest
with me naked!

Now, I've written this naked-in-the-hope-chest stuff as a
short story for the page, but there is something about my naked

body in real time in the theater crammed into that hope chest on the stage that totally changes, deepens the text. It gets the words sweaty! As long as I don't get splinters in my butt, that's what I want to do! Get those words to become FLESH!

Why I Spill the Autobiographical Beans

As good as all this sounds (I hope)—that my solo narratives carry with them the potential for creating community and shared agency—I know from first-hand experience the delights, dangers, and limits of working in the first person. The main buffet table that I lay out as an artist comes from the juicy menu of post-feminist, post-punk, personal-is-political, autobiographical narrative. As someone who has spent my whole creative life writing and performing stories from my experience, the tricky terrain of auto-biography is both a favorite comfy chair and a particularly scary attic room. I have bounced between the exquisite pleasures and the pitfalls that are inevitably part of the encounter with one's life and memory. I have put myself (and, of course, my boyfriends) through the most detailed public revelations of the psychic, emotional, and sexual personal narratives that flesh is heir to. I sometimes have to remind myself that not everyone could tolerate their lives being on display like this. Most people sensibly maintain some pretty fixed boundaries about what is and is not available for public consumption. Forget the aforementioned kiss-and-tell business—to rim-and-tell (look it up) loudmouths like me, these boundaries just function as a tempting dare to dive into what I hope might be a deeper, more-naked-than-skin truth.

I have kept a journal consistently since I was in fifth grade. The fact that I first picked up a spiral notebook at the age of ten and began writing daily about what happened to me is a hugely important fact of my life. Every bit as important as the fact that when I was fourteen I realized that I was gay, and that it was my fate to love the boy next door. I would hazard that my obsessive need as a boy-child to document *my* story was tightly bound up with the inchoate inkling that I would soon also have to rewrite *their* story, the heterosexual narrative! Naturally, a rewrite wasn't enough. It was just one flouncy leap from writing these stories down to performing them as a means of claiming identity with a public witness. Long before I began going to school dressed like Oscar Wilde when I was fifteen—an early conceptual, durational performance piece that was inspired by a play about Wilde on PBS's *Theater in America*—the impulse to tell my stories was my first declaration to the world that I was here and before too long would also be queer.

My favorite book during that revelatory Wildean sophomore year of high school was *The Confessions of Jean-Jacques Rousseau*. (This should have tipped everyone off right then that I was destined to be a naked, queer performance artist!) I suppose I was inspired by Rousseau's urgent need in his *Confessions* to spill all the beans: his obsessive masturbation, his penchant for indecent exposure in public parks, and so on. I learned that as salubrious as it is to spill those garbanzos in the privacy of your own Pee-Chee folder, it's even better to spread them out à la carte, to perform them for all to see. Since the moment I did my first feverish scribblings in my gay boy's adolescent journal—the crazed scrawl as panicky as a seismograph after an 8.1 earthquake—I have always seen writing about my life to be a fundamental act of knowing myself, of claiming space, and of simple survival. The act of remembering and sharing that memory with others became a crucial way to survive the shit that the world would strew in my path. As an adolescent I figured that if Rousseau's autobiographical ranting could start the French Revolution, my own might at least get me through high school so I could finally find a boyfriend. During the rigors of individuating as a gay boy in hate-filled America, I had somehow begun to believe that the act of writing and performing about my life just might be a way to find the potential to transform it. If the truth be told, I have never stopped believing this. Telling these life stories in my performances has always carried the potential for transforming my reality.

There is such a sweet hopelessness in trying to write from your life, a built-in certainty that whatever you cull will not be as layered or true as what any of us goes through in a single day. How can I hope in my performances to get at the knotty tendons of how complex real life actually is? Every time I try to tell a story from my life, I am pulling the words out through a shrinking device that makes the feelings and the experience and the joys and the shit seem all vaguely squeezed. It's as if you were trying to coax the last bit of toothpaste (or K-Y for that matter!) out of the tube and onto your trembling toothbrush (or red-purple cock). Like Pepe Le Pew forever caught in the grip of a Warner Bros. cartoon laundry wringer, I am in for trouble every time I start to tell a story about what has gone on in my life.

I know that the words I squeeze out of the tube and onto the page and finally onto the stage will never be as true or wet as the messy experiences as they are lived from day to day. Inevitably, the act of writing will distill, edit, change, compress, compact, alter, disguise, enhance, and reduce the raw mess of living. But parallel to that is another magic trick at work. As real as those perils are, the story from life can also hone, expose, reveal, connect, and dig up something from inside me that I can use to build a future. I know all too well that any arrangement of subjects and verbs I might find to describe my life story may well be insufficient by comparison to the actual wet feeling of the real thing, yet I know I must keep trying to find these words, write them, fling them from the stage and the page, or I will go fucking nuts from anger and fear.

Pushing beyond my more extravagant storytelling habits (my mix-master metaphors, attraction to puns, and shameless hyperbole, for starters), I want to find the words that might invite you into this place where I live. I perform these stories in the hope that someone else just might understand what it has felt like to

xxvi / BODY BLOWS

walk around in my smelly shoes. Contrary to the notion that auto-biographical storytelling is a closed system, I actually think that when I tell a story about *my* first kiss, the audience knows their main job is to recall the story of their first kiss. The intimacy of the direct-to-the-audience first-person address gives permission for everybody to sift through their inner snapshot album. Free from the totalizing conceit of realistic theater, my telling of my life stories is primarily a challenge for the audience to remember their own narratives. On a good day I can hold these stories out to them in the palm of my hand, in a clear light, as a shiny mirror to look into.

A User's Manual for This Book

Some Golden States, the show that begins the volume, is not my first piece. It was preceded by six full-evening works that were all developed between 1980 and 1986 at Performance Space 122 in New York City, the arts center I co-founded in 1980 with Charles Dennis, Charles Moulton, and Peter Rose. These included my earliest work, created at the age of twenty-one, a lean-and-mean, queer-punk vision called *Paint Yrself Red/Me & Mayakovsky,* which grandly connected my Southern California suburban child-hood to the great Soviet playwright and revolutionary. The next year I collaborated with my new boyfriend John Bernd on an ongoing performance project called *Live Boys,* about meeting, falling in love, and breaking up. A life-as-art process which no one should try without adult supervision. Since I came to New York City as a dancer, my work *Postwar* (1982) combined crazed move-ment, complex multimedia, a little text, and lawnmowers to explore the anomie and horror of growing up in nuclear America as it collided with the first Reagan term, when we all imagined he was going to blow up the world at any minute. I got a tremen-dous amount of international attention for this work, which puffed up my twenty-three-year-old self to no end and led me to my Hollywood period: my bloated, though well-intentioned,

Postwar, 1982

interdisciplinary spectacle *Cost of Living* (1983), and my mega-big-budget flop at the Brooklyn Academy of Music Next Wave Festival, *Democracy in America* (1984).

I felt washed-up at the age of twenty-six and moped around in my bathrobe for a few weeks groping for support from my boyfriend Doug Sadownick, my life partner from 1982 to 1995, and the outside eye and frequent composer for these early works. Finally with *Buddy Systems* (1986), the chastened Wunderkind came back to a high-energy, stripped-down performance that relied on words, storytelling, and physical performance to make some sparks as I told a bittersweet story of gay love—my relationship with Doug and our new dog Buddy. With AIDS rattling the windows, I knew I had a big job to do as a queer artist. I did not assume that I would live to see the age of thirty. It was at this point in my journey that my concerns, social vision, and performance inclinations really jelled. Doug and I moved to Los Angeles and I took off a big bite to chew with *Some Golden States.*

The earlier works were lively, risk-taking, and exploratory. They did not rely so much on text to carry the oomph of the performance, so I have not included them in this volume. However, along with my two tossed-salad "best of" shows, also not in this collection, *Sex/Love Stories* (1990) and the medley program based on my book of memoirs, *Shirts & Skin* (1997), I recall all these performances with great fondness and discernible tumescence.

This book starts with my first really confident, narrative, writerly piece, *Some Golden States* (1987), a tale of being cast from paradise into the world. *Stretch Marks* (1989), the second piece, pulls me toward the beginning of a personal-meets-political ACT UP worldview. I make my grab at the big shamanic brass ring in *My Queer Body* (1992), which describes my descending into the underworld and managing to find my way back. *Naked Breath* (1994) reveals a more intimate and quieter way of relating to AIDS, my history, and a single street in Manhattan. There's a joyful tribute to first sex/first love in *Fruit Cocktail* (1996). Finally, *Glory Box* (1999), about the struggle for gay marriage and immigration rights, connects my strongest writing, sharpest humor, and most emotional expression. In *Glory Box* I focus on the scary challenges my partner Alistair (who's from Australia) and I have been going through these last seven years to keep him in the United States, a country that denies all gay couples the immigration rights that all heterosexual married couples are afforded.

The performances included in this book are the shows I have been presenting all over the world for the last fifteen years. They mark a queer boy's progress through a Whittier childhood, falling in love, learning German from a Mexican lesbian in high school, confronting HIV-AIDS, surviving earthquakes, learning about relationships, challenging the state apparatus, growing fruit, falling naked into a volcano, and facing being forced to leave his country to stay with the man he loves. All this and jokes too! I feel lucky to have had all the performances documented by the extraordinary New York City photographer Dona Ann McAdams, a lifelong friend and co-conspirator. Dona's photos bring the breath, the body, the sweat, and the real-time heat of the performances to these pages.

Here We Go

In my performances I hope I have tried to dig as deep as I can at the things in my life that make me bang my head against the wall. All my work as a performer, writer, teacher, and activist has consistently tried to find the connections between my personal story and what happens in the society I inhabit. Jumping off into the deep end from the autobiographical diving board, I urgently look for the links between my words and my body, between my heart and my head, between my personal life and the world around me, between myself and the audience. I want to shake the trees and create community through the weird and exciting reality of performing.

I confess I have a completely unsubstantiated faith that if I tell my stories, I may be able to affect how the narrative will end. I have always used the memories of things past to rewrite the ending of what is to come. I have done this from that first moment that I picked up my Pee-Chee folder at the age of ten, wrote a play, and somehow knew that the queer boy star of my story was not going to end up hanging by his neck from a beam in our family's detached suburban garage. I tell these stories of who I have been to imagine who I might become. Even now as I write this introduction, knowing that my beloved Alistair and I will probably be forced very soon to leave this troubled nation, I tell my stories in these performances as a fierce act of imagining our future.

Tim Miller
millertale@aol.com
http://hometown.aol.com/millertale/timmiller.html

Body Blows

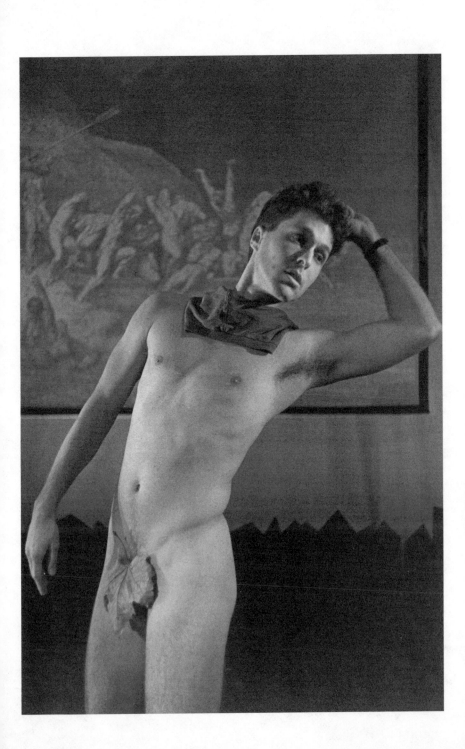

Some Golden States

Where do I begin?

Las Vegas lounge singers and performance artists always ask ourselves this question when we decide how to get started— whether it's crooning at the piano for the late set in the Rainbow Room or choosing what the new performance art piece will explore. I hope when I look that query in the eye I have consistently dared to face what is most urgent in my life.

I created *Some Golden States* in 1987. I was twenty-eight, and my world was in complete chaos. That year AIDS began to take its toll on my closest personal circle with the first deaths of people who were my friends and lovers. I was constantly haunted by my own fears that I would soon be next. As if we were catching the last plane out of Lisbon in 1940 to escape the Nazi's blitzkrieg, my partner Doug Sadownick and I had moved to LA fleeing the cold panic and tightening noose in New York. We made this move to improve the quality of our lives but also partly in the hope we would be less besieged by the plague in California's sunnier climes. That never works, does it?

That same year my hometown of Whittier, California, was devastated by an earthquake. Whittier, also the hometown of President Richard Nixon, has always existed as an archetypal place for me, somewhere off the interstate between Brecht's *Mahagony* and Wilder's *Our Town*. Faced with the post-earthquake reality of iconic sites such as the Whittier Cinema in ruins, I felt my personal cosmology further frayed. The world and my place in it were feeling very precarious indeed.

Some Golden States is about dirt, California dirt in particular. Where I come from the dirty earth still lives, moves, can shake your house down around you. It's the dirt in my metaphor-laden backyard—which makes frequent appearances in my work as a suburban Eden—that is the primal site of birth, growth, and killer tomatoes ready for the pasta. Dirt that I love, dirt that I plant seeds in, and rather naughtily in the show, dirt that I fuck as a horny teenager. With those grandiose intimations of mortality that your late twenties can bring even without a plague or earthquake in your vicinity, the piece is haunted by the dirt that we will all eventually become. My own first sober brushes with death are matched in the show by mortal blows to friends, heroes, idealism, and possibility.

The stage of *Some Golden States*—not to mention the wheelbarrow that sits down stage right—is strewn with the dirt into which I need to dig my toes as I commit myself to the joys and terrors of my times. Fecund and feisty, *Some Golden States* is an embarkation, a departure point for a self-conscious, queer Candide (moi!) about to be flung into the world. Like a resilient road-company Peter Pan who flies effortlessly on Flying-by-Foy wires only to splat against plague and catastrophe at the stage right wall, I manage to pick myself up and walk back onstage because I, along with my community, clearly do believe in fairies.

On the deepest level, *Some Golden States* was an effort to find an incantation, a prayer, a whistle in the dark if nothing else, to keep myself in the world. As someone who never met a metaphor I didn't like, this performance is the piece where I willfully plant my young man's feet deep in the earth with every intention of sticking around and making my garden grow.

(The lights come up on Tim lying in a pile of dry leaves by an old suitcase. There is a wheelbarrow on the right of the stage. Radio announcements about the 1987 Whittier, California, earthquake blare over slowed-down, ominous, scary-movie music. Tim strips off his clothes and humps the earth, his own private earthquake. Moves toward the wheelbarrow doing garden gestures: plant, hoe, harvest. For once, Tim puts a fig leaf over his dick. It takes some finagling with a paper clip. The sound collage peaks as images from Gustave Dore's engravings of Dante's Inferno *fill the upstage wall. Tim dresses, shakes the dirt-filled wheelbarrow, and shouts . . .)*

EARTHQUAKE!
PESTILENCE!
PLAGUE!
MORE EARTHQUAKES!

What a time it has been. It has not been a Garden of Eden. Everybody is always talking about gardens. Garden this. Garden that. Garden fresh. Garden sweet. Garden pure. Everybody is always talking about gardens like they're these perfect places. Where we know what we're supposed to do. Where nothing bad ever happens. Where people don't get sick and die. Where nobody gets their brains beaten in. Gardens are a place where everything fits: the carrot into its carrot hole, the bee into the blossom, the tomato into the pasta. There is an order to things. It's a place where you plant the seeds, you water the apricot, the sun shines, and they grow and you eat them and live. I guess you still have to die in this arrangement.

BUT NOT RIGHT NOW.

I think this probably all started with this Garden of Eden business. That's what put the idea in our heads that there is this perfect place that we've been cast out from. Now everyone's trying to find their way back. All these people like Ulysses, the Flying Dutchman, Candide, and E.T. They're all trying to find their way home. To some place in a garden. Where we can be and live?

Well, I dunno. I dunno if there is any place like that. No Garden of Eden. No Garden of Allah. And definitely no Garden of Earthly Delights. No perfect place.

I know there's no place like that.

I'm sure there's no place like that.

I believe there's no place like that.

But I've probably been trying to find it anyway. Some good spot where I can be and live and call it . . . home?

(Tim pulls out a brown bag and begins to plant fully grown vegetables in the wheelbarrow soil.)

I have a garden. Right now in California I have a garden in Los Angeles and I *know* that's no Garden of Eden. The smog. The earthquakes. The tomato bugs have been very bad this year. My boyfriend Doug recently got beaten up by somebody with a two-by-four on his way home at night. It's *no* Garden of Eden. But, nevertheless, I have my garden there. With carrots, broccoli, tomatoes, and zucchini.

And that's my garden. I try to make the plants grow. I water this garden a lot. I like watering. You just turn on your faucet and you squirt everything with the hose. It immediately looks better and you're convinced it's grown an inch. It washes all the dirt off and it looks fresh and clean. But it's not only my vegetables that I like watering. I also like watering the sides of buildings, the driveway, my ceiling . . . my self. You water yourself and these other things, you just point your hose at stuff and it looks better.

Wet and refreshed and slippery and clean. It looks better. Well, at least till it dries, if you know what I mean.

This isn't my first garden. I've had others. When I was a teenager in Whittier, California, I had a big garden with vegetables. I'd been reading a lot of Tolstoy at the time, especially his stuff from his weirded out later years when he thought everyone should just work the earth and make food grow. This made a lot of sense to me. So I started a big vegetable garden and grew carrots, broccoli, tomatoes, and zucchini.

I sat there in that garden. I wanted my garden to teach me the things I didn't know. Things I wanted to get. I guess I should have been satisfied with huge red tomatoes and obscenely large zucchini (more on that later). But I wanted more from my garden. I wanted a model of the world, the image and the outline of some place that works. Everything would be in its place there. The dirt, the water, the sun, the growth, the life.

I would sit in my garden and love the dirt under my fingernails, and on my skin, and between my toes. I watched things grow and got ready to go into the world. I waited for the big wisdom to come. There among the carrots, broccoli, tomatoes, and zucchini.

(As the piano music fades, Tim does the garden gestures again very slowly and then pulls himself up to announce the first section.)

IN WHICH THE YOUNG TIM PREPARES TO LEAVE HIS HOME IN WHITTIER FOR THE VERY FIRST TIME!

(Tim runs to the suitcase and sits. The maudlin whine of the strings from Aaron Copland's Appalachian Spring *comes over the sound system. Tim will be accompanied by this music, speaking in time with it, for the rest of the section. Be assured that Tim will squeeze all the gorgeous campy sentimentality he can out of the music.)*

I had packed my bags. I was nineteen. It was the night before I was going to leave my home for the very first time. It was a young time. It was a simpler time. I was there in the backyard of the house I had grown up in there in Whittier, California. I was in my garden, in my carrot patch, and I stood there . . .

I was a blooming bud of California, ready to leave the branch and go to seek my home state. This state. My state.

When I was a kid, when I wondered where I was, when I was lost and alone and I wondered where my home was, I would ask myself, "Where do I live? Where is my home?" And I would answer with this list: "I live in my bedroom, in my parents' house, on Pounds Avenue, in the city of Whittier, in the state of California, in the United States, in North America, in the Western hemisphere, on the planet Earth, in the solar system, in the Milky Way galaxy, in the universe!"

I would ask myself this question about where my home was and I would answer with this list. Because if you repeat the list very fast you start to believe it. To believe you know where your home actually is. I had packed my bags. I was nineteen. It was the night before I was going to leave my home for the very first time.

I was a tender sapling of California, erect and arching and stretching into the night!

I looked up and heaved a long sigh . . .

(Tim heaves a long sigh.)

. . . and wondered what moves man hither and thither, like those stars in the firmament above as they wander in their stately and permanent parade.

I'M LEAVING MY HOME! I'M LEAVING MY HOME! I'M LEAVING MY HOME!!!!

What is this mysterious motion that moves me as it moved my great-great-great-grandfather from his humble mill in Germany to come to rural New York just in time for the Civil War. Then on to Kansas for a generation or two and finally . . . OH

CORN-CHEWING GRANDPARENTS!!! who trekked west in 1919 to California across the burning desert until at last they huffed and puffed over Cajon Pass. They greeted the Promised Land with a bold and lusty cry as they kissed the rich earth of the Los Angeles Basin. Here my parents would meet and find their way to the green and sensual hills of Whittier where they and their like would sire me and my kind . . .

A NEW AND A COURAGEOUS RACE OF CALIFOR-NIANS!

At last El Dorado has been found! Far from ancient Europe and the icy northern past, a golden state full of hope and promise, year-round tanning and Mexican fast food!

And that confident cry of "EUREKA!" ejaculated from their lips, rejoicing that the ever-westering civilization had at last found the sea—the sea that stretched to the mysterious Asian east and the spicy Latin south—where the cultures and the freeways meet . . . calling us home, ever home.

I had packed my bags. I was nineteen. It was the night before I was going to leave my home for the very first time.

I was a fertile flower of California. Heavy with a musky pollen and ready to be plucked!

What was calling me away that night? What was pulling me on? Driving me that night from home and hearth, from kith and kin? And I raised my fist to an unkind power above that would soon exile me from paradise and swore by every shimmering light in the panoply above that "I WOULD FIND MY WAY BACK!!!"

As Odysseus to Ithaca, so would I to Whittier. With this vow I grasped a handful of that California land and cast it to the stars!!! I felt a new and vibrating pillar of life grow forcefully inside of me.

I was a ripe fruit of California, juicy and throbbing, and bulging with unimagined, unforeseen, and fantastic possibilities!

(Tim pulls out a human-sized cutout of the state of California and begins to make love to it. These "home" issues need to be worked out at some point, right?)

I wanted to join with that earth, my California land, and somehow find a way to make sweet and passionate love with that home that had spawned me. With every rounded mound and craggy peak. From Mount Shasta to Salton Sea. With every town and hamlet, from Weed in the north to Needles in the south. To caress them, to become one. To pierce at last this deep longing for a place.

(The piece starts to get nasty here as Tim starts to fuck the state of California.)

I felt my swollen hardness pulsating at my loins, desiring to enter, to penetrate my backyard in Whittier! What could I do? How could I consummate this pointed passion? And in the heat of my need it came to me; I pulled a stout carrot from my carrot patch and thrust it into the still sun-warmed, moist, pungent earth. I needed to make a nest, a tight hole, in which my six (and five-eighths) inches of WASP dick—don't laugh, it's a new concept—could at last find a sweet home, soothing comfort, angelic release!

I let loose that massive throbbing pillar from my straining trousers, fell to the ground, and pressed my body to the earth as I slowly entered my backyard in Whittier. Squishing past slug and worm, their congeal lubricating this tender congress, this dear commingling! I licked each leaf of green with my searching tongue, nibbling insatiably at seed and sage. Again and again and again I slid into the earth with greater and greater force. In and out.
LOVING THE CALIFORNIA LAND.
PLOWING THE CALIFORNIA LAND.
ONE WITH THE CALIFORNIA LAND.
PLANTING MY SEED IN THE CALIFORNIA LAND!
And at that moment, as I neared my pleasure-soaked pinnacle, my thoughts went back to Grandma and Grandpa and the ecstatic look on their faces as they first gazed past the Colorado River toward the new life that was laid out before them. With that

vision hovering before me, I made a vow, a vow that promised this:

(Tim is humping the state wildly.)

Though someday soon I shall leave you, Sweet California, I swear I shall return! I shall find my way back to you! Wherever I go, this loyal son of yours, wherever I may wander, I shall carry you with me. It may take a year, or ten, or my whole life, but I will come back to you!

CALIFORNIA . . . HERE . . . I . . . COME!

(The music peaks and Tim comes. Blackout. Lights fade up on the wheelbarrow, where Tim does the gardening dance again . . . a little bigger this time.)

IN WHICH THE OVER-IDEALISTIC TIM TRIES TO FIND A BETTER WORLD AND INSTEAD DISCOVERS A MISTY ABYSS OF DECEIT, SUBTERFUGE, AND DEATH.

(Tim runs to "hitchhike" area and sticks his thumb out.)

I was hitchhiking. Out of Bakersfield. Up Highway 99.

My thumb, which had been up someone's butt the night before, is out.

My thumb is out. My body is young. My heart is pure. I'm emotionally completely fucked up.

And I need a ride pronto.

I am going to San Francisco for a few days. I'm nineteen. It's 1978. I'm a post-punk Southern California kid. I'd missed out on the big hippie thing by about ten years, but I felt the weight of that previous generation's nostalgia as heavy as a truckload of Woodstock albums crashing again and again into my face. But big things seem to be happening up in SF. There's this new mayor, a good guy named Moscone. Plus this guy named Harvey Milk, who is a fag like me, has just gotten elected to citywide office. I sent his campaign thirty-eight dollars I saved from my lawn mowing jobs.

They sent me this cool T-shirt that says "Harvey Milk *Super*visor." It feels like a revolution or something, a better world about to happen. El Dorado. The Grail. The Perfectible Social Order. This could be the start of something big! So, I'm on my way to check it out. I have an address of a friend of a friend of a friend and twelve dollars in my pocket. I'm not nearly as smart as I think I am but at least I am starting to realize this.

My thumb is out. The cars swoop past.

Woooosh. Shit. Wooosh. Fuck! Woooosh. Fucking shit! ErrrrrrrH.

At last a ride in a 1974 canary yellow Pinto! I throw my backpack in the back and two hours later I find myself at the corner of Powell and Market Street.

I walk down Market Street with my backpack on my back. I look at everything I see with a face that is an open wallet.

(Tim does a callow, Pollyanna-ingenue walk.)

Within ten minutes, I had been kidnapped by the Moonies, thrown on a bus, and was heading over the Golden Gate Bridge, destination unknown.

Well, I hadn't actually been kidnapped and I swear to you I didn't know they were Moonies. They came up to me and said, "Hello. We're from the Creative Cooperative Community Project, a progressive, forward-looking communal organization working toward a new world order. Please come for a free meal at our utopian farm."

Well, it sounded great to me. I mean, I thought they were Stalinists. Creative Cooperative Community Project! CCCP! It seemed pretty clear. I'd had two weeks of Russian. Plus I had been hitchhiking for sixteen hours, had twelve dollars in my pocket, and the offer of a ride on a bus with free food sounded pretty good. Plus, isn't this the kind of thing that's supposed to happen your first ten minutes in San Francisco? So off I went.

Now, on the bus, there was indeed a lot of food. But it was all kind of strange food. It was all made with broccoli. In fact, it was all made with wilted broccoli. The million little nubs were all droopy and yellow. There are wilted broccoli sandwiches. Wilted broccoli casserole. Wilted broccoli Danish!!!! What does all this wilted broccoli mean?

I grow skeptical. But this is a progressive, forward-looking communal organization working toward a new world order! So I load up my plate, eat myself silly, and fall asleep. Three hours later, the bus creaks and grinds over a dirt road 140 miles north of SF and I embark on eight hours of indoctrination, calisthenics, and camp songs. The next morning there's this schlumpy guy at a blackboard who is explaining everything to us. The function of good and bad in the universe. The ultimate evil of communism. How man and woman can be happy and complete only through marriage. And, finally, and most inexplicably, how his interpretation of the book of Revelation in the Bible clearly shows how the second coming of Jesus Christ can only be from South Korea!

I grow more skeptical.

But I finally lose it when we're out on the playing fields during one of our many exercise breaks. They're having us play volleyball. Now I don't want anyone to think this is an anti-sports show. Volleyball is one of the least objectionable of all sports, almost a homosexual sport. Volleyball wasn't the problem. BUT . . . they wanted us to chant "WIN WITH LOVE!" while we play. Even as a native Californian I found this very challenging. I tried. Win with love . . .

(Tim serves.)

Win with love

(Tim returns the ball.)

Win with love!

(Spike and point.)

Look! Time out! I don't think I'm cut out to be a member of a cult. I have an appointment with someone in the Haight in just two hours, a homosexual gentleman who will probably suck my dick! So if someone would get me my backpack and sleeping bag and then drive me back to San Francisco?

There was complete silence on the playing field. People started to whisper. Someone ran off toward the main building. The dogs were let loose and a siren began to wail. Then, three of the creepiest of these characters came up to me and said, "Don't go. Don't go. Stay. Sleep on it! It's getting late. Stay! Stay!"

I pulled away. They were scaring me. They had something behind their backs. What were those things? They were greenish. They were glowing. They were . . . heads of broccoli. These were not merely ordinary heads of broccoli. These were not merely ordinary heads of wilted broccoli. No, these broccoli heads had minds and souls and faces. Stolen spirits of optimistic young people! This was the attack of the broccoli brain suckers and I shouted, "BACK! I am the Antichrist. I am a communist. I am a fag!" What else can I say to scare them away?

"Get me my backpack and sleeping bag or I'll call the police!!!!"

Well, POLICE was the magic word. About one second later, they got me my stuff and kicked me out onto the dirt road. My thumb instinctively went out. I was breathing fast. I looked around. The world was still there. Everything seemed to be okay. I knew I had come through something big. Some weird kind of trial by vegetable. And now I was back in the world, where I would have to figure out stuff by myself. My thumb was out.

This began about two-and-a-half magic hours of hitchhiking. Where each ride is followed by the next one and every driver offers their bit of gem-like wisdom. Instantly an Armenian schoolteacher in a pickup truck pulled to a halt, shoved open the door and said, "Quick, kid, get in before they change their minds." He drove me down the mountain and told me, "Kid, forget that Moonie business, ya gotta follow your own star! Promise me you'll follow your own star!!!" He dropped me off at Highway 101. Instantly four hippies in a beat-up old Saab pulled over. All four doors opened and I was pulled in. They graciously got me stoned while reading to me my favorite passages from Hermann Hesse's Buddha novel *Siddhartha* along the way. They left me at Santa Rosa. Immediately an Episcopalian priest picked me up. He started telling me about his wife and kids with his hand stroking the inside of my thigh the whole way. During this ride I learned more than I ever wanted to know about the Anglican communion. He left me off in Mill Valley. Finally, there was the cute boy from Marin County, who drove me the rest of the way. At last, we rounded those headlands and I saw the Golden Gate and San Francisco beyond. I wanted to grab each one of those bridge towers, tap dance down those bridge cables back into my world . . .

. . . and my second day in San Francisco!

(Tim falls flat on his back. Morning light streams in.)

I woke up the next morning on my friend of a friend of a friend's hardwood floor. He had been arrested for doing fifteen-dollar back-alley blow jobs on Polk Street. His housemates were not amused by my knock on their door at 1 A.M. Or by my big tale of "I ESCAPED FROM THE MOONIES!" They looked at me like I was the most naive idiot who had ever gotten taken in by the oldest scam on Market Street. I got out of there quick. I wandered around North Beach as the direct-from-central-casting fog rolled in. I felt so depressed. So disillusioned. What had I expected? What did I want from this place? I think what I really wanted was to have Allen Ginsberg come bursting out of City Lights Bookstore and say "Tim! You made it! Congrats! Kid, lemme buy ya a latte!"

Since Allen Ginsberg was nowhere to be found, I thought going to the beach might cheer me up. So I got on the bus and I headed out to Land's End.

(Mood lights please and a little haunting music as Tim walks along the very edge of the stage, marking the coastline.)

This is the edge. The edge of a continent. The edge of Western civilization. Land's End. It was very beautiful here. Waves crashing. Sky above. Seals barking on the rocks. Fluffy clouds shaped like toaster ovens and Scottish terriers floating overhead. I see a beach at the bottom of the cliff. It's about the size of a compact parking space. It has two hundred people on it.

I climb down to this Geo Metro–size beach and I see it is homo nude-beach-arama here. I have no hang-ups, right? So, I take off my clothes, hide my money, and start doing my modern dance animal impressions that I had been learning: the Scurrying Squirrel, the Stately Heron, the Pensive Possum. I climb over one rock and I see a vision. A beautiful naked man dipping his foot in the cold, cold sea. It was Caravaggio on parade! He looked at me and smiled. I almost fainted. To impress him I jump in the water, walk toward him, and immediately lose all sensation below my neck.

He shouts to me, "Hey! Isn't the water cold?" My mind races. What does he mean cold? Does he mean cold in an emotional sense? "I ... umm ... oh!" Listen to me! I sound like a lunatic. Look at this guy. He's so confident, so sure of himself. How did he get like that? He pulls me out of the water and we sit together and talk. His name is Michael. He's a student at San Francisco State. He's taking a class on James Joyce. I look out of the corner of my eye and I see that he has an open copy of James Joyce's *Portrait of the Artist as a Young Man* there on his knee. I have to tell you that both then and now, this seemed to me to be the height of sexiness to sit next to this naked man at the edge of a continent with that book open on his oh so tan knee. It even looked like he'd read a couple pages!

We talk for a while, the ocean at our feet. I want Michael to think I'm smart so I try to use the word "semiotic" to describe Molly Bloom's sexuality in *Ulysses*. I think I fucked it up because he looks at me like I'm an idiot and says he better go. Wait, before he goes (don't judge me, it worked) he gives me his phone number, writes it on my arm in magic marker, and tells me to call him later and maybe we'll have dinner at the Socialist Gay Men's Collective where he lives. He puts on his clothes, climbs up the hill, and disappears along the path.

Two hours later, I'm walking down Fulton Street toward City Hall. I want to see the building where this guy Harvey Milk is changing the world. Well, at least my world. At least for now. I've called my friend Michael and we are going to have dinner later at his house in the Sunset District. I have bought the Cliffs Notes for *Finnegans Wake* so I can bone up before dinner.

He asks me, "What shall I make for us for dinner? Do you like broccoli?"

I say, "Sure, I love broccoli."

Finally I get to City Hall and I look at this big building and I think why is this building so big? It looks like it could be the capitol of an empire of something, not just a city hall. I look at this fat building and I feel a fat joy. Because there I am, a young idiot, with James Joyce in my hand and a date for dinner. All this, but also the feeling of the wheels of the state grinding begrudgingly in concert with me. There's this guy Harvey Milk, a fag like me, in there ruffling the corduroys of power! I feel so strong. I feel like I'm in the Paris Commune. With my German ancestors in Dresden in the 1848 uprising storming the barricades. I feel for once that the world is not an enemy, that society *is* perfectible and I HAVE A DATE FOR DINNER!!!

As I walk away from City Hall, I think to myself, "Well, I only have three dollars left. I guess I'll have to go back to Whittier for a while. Unless Michael asks me to marry him and move in at the Socialist Gay Men's Collective. But I want to come back here some day and make a life here in this city. But, for now, I go off to my broccoli.

A few months later, I'm working a stupid job at a gas station near Disneyland. I'm pumping someone's gas and I overhear this conversation.

Some jerk says, "Hey, dya hear the news. They got those two guys up in Frisco. Yeah, some cop killed that queer Milk and that dago commie mayor of theirs ... whatshisname ... Macaroni?"

I dropped the gas nozzle to my side.

I knew it was time to leave California.

I am covered in gasoline.

(Music and lights fade as Tim goes to wheelbarrow and does garden dance sequence again, more urgently this time.)

IN WHICH THE INCREASINGLY SKEPTICAL TIM TRIES TO FIND AN APARTMENT IN NEW YORK CITY!

(Sound effects of a jet plane taking off. Tim scoots to suitcase and sits on the airplane. Vibrations shake his body and he begins to fly across stage. Tim does wild dance to gloppy fifties hi-fi music, Manhattan Tower. *Tim stomps floor and prepares to list his New York City apartments.)*

Right here!

Right here!

I arrive on a nonstop flight from LAX to JFK and I arrive right here! At the corner of Twenty-third and Eighth Ave. I spend the next three days at the International Ladies' Garment Workers' Union Building at *Twenty-third and Eighth*.

With a friend of a friend of a friend. I have a three-day limit. I, like bad fish, must leave. I walk the streets and quickly discover

that everyone is so friendly in New York! Especially if you're nineteen and have a great butt!

I meet this Irish-American guy on the street. I move to *Second Avenue and Tenth Street*. He lives right across from the Second Avenue Deli. I spend the next five days bouncing up and down on an Irish man's dick from New Jersey. While he fucks me, I can see them across the street carving the lox so thin "you could read the *New York Times* through it!" Things get too tight.

I get a roommate off of a bulletin board and I move to *13 Saint Mark's Place*. I move in with an insane novelist cabdriver just out of Harvard. He is desperate for Puerto Rican boys. He is always being cited by the Taxi and Limousine Commission for giving blow jobs in the back of his cab on his breaks. The day I move in, Con Ed turns off the electricity. (He hadn't paid the bill in five months.) For fiscal security, I decide to move downtown . . .

(Tim runs in to the audience.)

. . . all the way downtown. I move to *393 Broadway*. OH BEAUTIFUL BROADWAY! This is Broadway! This is White Street. Catty-corner to what will soon be the mondo hipoid club the Mudd Club later that year.

I move in with four really terrible painters just out of art school. We divide two thousand square feet of raw space and five hundred dollars a month five ways. We build rooms out of packing crates and a bunch of fabric I found on Lispenard Street. During this time, I am always bringing home stray dogs, stray cats, STRAY ATTRACTIVE CHILEAN REFUGEES!

(Tim runs back onstage.)

During this time, I am also spending my nights basically at *64 Wooster Street* with my boyfriend of that time trying to make this guy love me. The plot thickens. He wants to move in with me at . . .

(Tim runs in to the audience. Again.)

. . . *393 Broadway!* That's beautiful Broadway. But there are already twelve people living there.

He drives my housemates mad. They say he has to go. I say, "If he goes, I go!" I go.

(Tim runs back onstage. At last.)

In fact, I go all the way back to California never to return to New York again. But then this same boyfriend snaps his finger via a postcard and I go running back. So cheap, so easy!

I move in to *153 Norfolk Street.* Three rooms. Two hundred and fifty dollars a month with a view of the Empire State Building thirty-three blocks and three economic classes away from me. That same boyfriend finally asks me to move in with him right up the block at . . . *184 Norfolk Street!* And I think, "Oh thank God, at last. Living together! Victory is Mine!" But it doesn't work out. We almost kill each other. He has a nervous breakdown and goes to Poland. I'm not kidding. He's there enjoying the wild nightlife of Warsaw while I'm stuck in dull as dishwater Manhattan. My life is in a ruin, a shambles, chaos! As I often do when my life is in a ruin, shambles, chaos . . . I get a new boyfriend and spend some time at *306 East Sixth Street.* Then I fuck up in a big way, but that, as they say, is a different story.

A friend is out of town and I move in to *309 East Fifth Street.* This is the perfect apartment. Three rooms. Five windows on the street. Corner of Second Avenue. On a block with a police station. For $110 a month!!! Am I in heaven? But I can't stay here. It's a sublet.

So, I move to *234 East Fourth Street,* at the corner of Avenue B, which from now on I will refer to only as "THE MAW OF DEATH!"

(Stage lights bump to lurid red.)

MAW, spelled M-A-W, meaning the gaping mouth of a slaughtered pig! (There's been confusion. People think I'm talking about a shopping center.) This building came equipped with numerous drug dealers, armed people in the hallways, and a very active Santería chapter. Which in those culturally insensitive times seemed to me to be the Lower East Side version of voodoo meets the Virgin Mary. This particular Santería chapter was very big on blood ritual.

Often, I would come home and find the headless bodies or severed heads of PIGS! GOATS! CHICKENS! My friend Dona was gonna move in, but then someone carved a death's head on her door and hung a piece of pig intestine from her doorknob. Dona was smart. SHE DIDN'T MOVE IN! I am embarrassed to say, "I SIGNED A LEASE FOR THE MAW OF DEATH!"

Family of twelve next door. Punk rock band above. And a trendy boy named Martin to my left. He was blond. With a vengeance. Martin would prove to be the one good thing I would find in the Maw of Death. The day I moved in, there was a fire in the building next door. It was an abandoned building, but it was being used by junkies as a shooting gallery. Now, as the fire got worse, the junkies started throwing themselves out the windows, scampering down the red-hot fire escapes. They looked like roaches jumping out of a toaster in summertime when you turn it on or shake it. I looked out my window as I hung my Peter Pan curtains and thought, "Gee, at last, a home of my own."

There was a knock at the door. Who could it be? It was Martin! He wanted to welcome me to the building. He was cute. Beefy muscles (unusual for 1981). Great smile. Four hundred earrings (even more unusual). And truly the most extreme post-punk multi-colored Mohawk-referenced haircut I had ever seen in my life. He invited me into his apartment. We looked at his paintings, for he was of course an artist—he designed record albums—and we did a large but not unreasonable amount of cocaine. Now, we could have fucked around right then. Via the usual neck rub–cocaine strategy. But we didn't. We just talked. And watched the fire burn the building down next door. And listened to our favorite song of that time, the Human League singing "These Are the Things That Dreams Are Made Of."

And that's how we met. And that's how we became friends. I would live next door to Martin at the Maw of Death for almost two years, and during that time many terrible things would happen.

Three people would kill themselves by jumping into the central airshaft of our building.

Once a week, Hector, our super, would run through the hallways pounding on our metal doors with his machete, cursing us in Spanish. Martin had to fight off a bunch of junkies when they tried to kill him but he kicked them in the face with his newly fashionable, New Romantic, hip-high, pirate boots.

Finally, most horrible of all, I went out on the stairwell one morning and saw hand smears of blood going all the way from the fourth floor to the first . . . ending in a more decisive pool by the torn-out mailboxes. There was something wrong with this building. Something terribly wrong. Have any of you ever seen the movie *Rosemary's Baby?* Well, it was like that, but without parquet floors, Mia Farrow, or Central Park views. Why live in the house of Satan without those three things? I couldn't take it anymore. I put my stuff in storage and left the country. I just counted myself lucky that I had broken my lease with the Maw of Death.

When I came back to New York, I found a new apartment. It was only eight feet wide. But it was on a good block, Mulberry between Prince and Spring in Little Italy. No light or cross-ventilation. But only $255 a month. I would have that apartment for many years. Also, at the same time I got a new boyfriend. This guy Doug, who made the keyboard music you're hearing over the sound system. I met Doug at a Christmas party on the Upper West Side. This party was attended mostly by queer performance artists from the East Village. I wore a red shirt to the party; these safety pins which used to be piercing my cheek and lip were now used only to hold up the trim, crisp, careerist sleeves of eighties New Wave New York! Doug arrived, a Bronx beauty. He looked like a Hebraic Jimmy Olsen boy reporter on Superman in his crisp bow tie. When Doug arrived a thought balloon appeared over the heads of all the queer performance artists that read "FRESH MEAT." I've always been quick, so I got there first and exchanged phone numbers and Doug and I began a big journey together.

But I keep going back. I keep thinking back to 234 East Fourth Street and Martin, the one good thing I found there. We didn't become good friends while we lived there. It was like we were already practically roommates, so we kept a kind of neighborly distance. It was only once we had both moved out of the Maw of Death that it felt like we could become better friends. And decide if we were going to fuck around in a serious fashion. We met again the summer after we had moved out of the Maw. We ran into each other on our bikes on Lower Broadway. We were so happy to see each other. We hugged and we hugged some more. Then our hands reached down to one another's butts and that was it.

Now it was August, and August is a very strange time in New York.

(Lights get steamy and augusty as music for midnight bike rides in Manhattan comes on.)

It is so hot. It is so humid. In August, it feels like life and time have stood still. It feels like everything is up for grabs. All the rules can be broken. And you can spend the entire month of August doing nothing but riding down Park Avenue South in the middle of the night riding your bike with no hands as you chase after a lunatic blond guy with a great butt spread on his bike seat as you race down the lower Twenties. I was twenty-four then, racing through my lower twenties. And I was glad to be on my bike this August in New York.

One night, we got on our bikes to catch a midnight movie on the Upper East Side. We raced around Grand Central Station and got there with just enough time to make out underneath a stoop of a building at Sixty-First and Second. Our hands diving into our pants like hungry fish. We didn't sleep together that night. I'm not sure why. Idiots.

The next day I called my friend Dennis, to ask him what he thought safe sex was. We were all sort of new at this then . . . in 1983. He said, "Oh yeah . . . hmmm . . . safe sex. I've got the *New York Native* here, let me check. I think we can do whatever we want but you're just supposed to do it with less people than we used to. Here it is. Oops, I got it wrong, it says whatever you do, don't suck, fuck, rim, or kiss him."

It was, and is, a complicated time. But it was complicated for other reasons too. See, I was already seeing my friend Doug. Nothing definite yet, but definitely on the verge. But he was off in Boston with an ex-boyfriend. Ex, but not so ex that he wouldn't still accept free trips to Jamaica from him.

So I was alone in New York in August. And I was much taken with my friend Martin and our wild rides uptown. Because we were Martin and Tim: The Two Who Had Escaped the Maw of Death!!!

The next day, it was so hot that we decided to blow off work . . . not that we had jobs. We made a plan to go to Brighton Beach. I had bought an inflatable surf-rider on Fourteenth Street so when we got there we blew up the surf-rider, got on it together, and floated way out beyond everybody else. We just bobbed there, told stupid jokes, kissed a little bit, showed each other our hard dicks under the waterline, and jerked each other off under the Atlantic as we waved to people back on the shore of Brooklyn. It felt so private. It felt like we were our own little surf-rider island floating there off the coast of America. It felt like we might never have to go back. We could just stay there on our surf-rider island. But we did have to go back. It was getting dark. So we paddled back in. Deflated the surf-rider. Got on the F Train. And headed back to Manhattan.

Now when we got back to Little Italy, it was still so hot that we headed straight for my apartment . . . took off our clothes and got in the shower together with only the cold water on and began making out in a serious way. Now this was very nice. Our bodies slick and hot from the sun and the sea. And we fucked and poked and swallowed and sucked and generally supped at each other's tables.

(Tim does frantic sex-in-the-shower gesture sequence.)

In case you're wondering, this is the internationally recognized physical action for sex in the shower. But as often happens when you try to have sex in the shower, there came a moment when the water began to feel too wet. I started to think, "Oh, Doug is coming back to New York tonight." I began to feel a little guilty. I'm like that sometimes—Mr. Guilt.

So I told Martin I thought we should stop. He knew what was going on. We got out of the shower. Dried off. Put on as little as possible, went out into the Mulberry Street night and walked and talked. Later that night . . . Doug came over and we fucked like nuts on the dirty carpeting of 241 Mulberry Street.

Later that year . . . Doug and I moved in together.

Later that year . . . I ran into Martin at Rockefeller Center and we had a very good talk.

The next year . . . I put Martin in a videotape I was doing.

The next year . . . I just caught a glimpse of Martin. On a new bike. Racing down Broadway. I knew things were going well in his life. He'd designed the record cover for his best friend Madonna's first American EP and he had an even more extreme and ambitious haircut.

The next year . . . Martin was dead. Of you-know-what.

(Tim spells AIDS in the air. Puts a period at the end.)

I had been out of New York a lot. Here in California. So I didn't hear about it when it happened. Didn't do the hospital time. It was only later a friend told me and I sat down on the street and said, "OH, Shit." That big blond body. The paintings. The bike riding. The life. It's like all nothing now.

Oh shit.
See, I thought we both had escaped the Maw of Death.
I was wrong.

(Ominous, slowed-down music lurches into the space. Tim shakes the wheelbarrow in another earthquake and shouts out the opening lines of the show again.)

EARTHQUAKE!
PESTILENCE!
PLAGUE!
ASSASSINATION!
MORE EARTHQUAKES!

(Tim does final crazed, out-of-control vegetable dance as earthquake, emergency, and AIDS alarms blare. Manic, climactic careening with the wheelbarrow around the stage. Dirt flies in the audience members' laps. Finally, Tim climbs in the wheelbarrow, buries his feet in the remaining dirt, and dangles a zucchini over his head. The audio collage fades out and only a quiet, bittersweet piano is playing.)

There once was this king. There was this Greek king long ago. And there was also this guy in the king's court named Damocles. Damocles was very jealous of the king and he went around saying, "Oh, oh, oh! The king is so lucky to be king. The king has it made. The king has everything made. Oh, oh, oh! How I wish that I were king."

Now the king heard about these things that Damocles was saying and he didn't like it very much. He wanted to teach Damocles a lesson so he invited him over for dinner. The king prepared Damocles a special seat at his dinner table. Damocles was very excited because he had gotten an invitation to have dinner with the king. Damocles put on his best toga, hopped in a cab, and went right over.

When Damocles got to the king's house he sat right down at his place at the table. He began to realize something was very wrong. He looked right. He looked left. Then he looked up and he saw that a very long, very sharp sword was hanging over his chair. It was hanging over his head by a single thread. It was hanging there, that sword of Damocles, and he knew that it could fall at any moment and crash through his head and crush his brains and then he would be dead. Damocles started to get up and change to another seat, but the king said, "Sit down! I thought you wanted to see what it felt like to sit at the king's table!" Damocles knew that he would have to sit there and eat his dinner. Looking up—every now and then—at that sword hanging over his head.

Of course, the king himself had hung that sword over Damocles' head. He was chuckling about this as he ate his royal ancient Greek delicacies—his falafel and tahini combo platter—and he watched Damocles squirm. He was laughing because he wanted to teach Damocles a lesson about the vulnerability of life. He wanted Damocles to know that at any moment for anybody, for everybody, whether you're the king or Damocles, there is a sword hanging over you by a thread. At any time it might come crashing down through your head.

Damocles finished his dinner—he ate a little more quickly than usual—then carefully eased himself out of his chair. He went up to the king to say good-night. Damocles was about to leave, but he went back to the king and thanked him, his eyes looking to the floor. Damocles walked home, through the streets, and got to his condo. He didn't go right inside. He went to his garden and sat down. Damocles looked up at the sky, the night. He thought about things, his life. As he sat there in the garden, there among his broccoli, his carrots, his tomatoes, his zucchini. Damocles thought about that sword that was still hanging over his head. He realized it was always there, even now in his garden. Damocles looked down and noticed one particularly large zucchini by

his right foot. He nudged it and pulled a bug off. He thought some more as he looked at this zucchini. That zucchini by his foot and over my head. That zucchini of Damocles is over my head now. It's as sharp as a sword and it might at any moment drop and squash through my brains. It hangs there by a single thread, that zucchini of Damocles.

And I go home. And I go in my gate. And I sit in my garden, there among my broccoli, my carrots, my tomatoes, my zucchini. And I look up at the sky, the night. I think about the same things as Damocles, my life. That zucchini hanging over my head by a single thread.

I think and I pull a couple of weeds. I water a little bit and pick a tomato to take it into the house for my boyfriend, Doug.

And I decide, right then and there, I decide to dig my toes deep into the dirt. I decide to plant my toes deep into the earth. I decide to plant my feet, to plant myself and to water myself. I will plant myself here in the earth, where I want to stick around, doing things, living and loving, in my life, in the world, in this garden.

I will plant myself in the world.
I will plant myself in the world.
I will plant myself in the world.
I will plant my self . . .
I will plant my self . . .
I will plant my self . . .

(The lights and music fade slow as Tim repeats these words, a chant, a prayer, an incantation. Standing there in the dirt in his wheelbarrow, a zucchini hanging over his head.)

Stretch Marks

While part of me can still admire the blithe chutzpah it takes to title a performance "Stretch Marks" at the callow age of thirty, from my current perspective it seems a little over-determined, a tiny bit drama-queeny around the edges! But the truth is that by the time I turned thirty, I did feel profoundly stretched. Stretched by the horrifying loss from AIDS of hundreds of people I had known. Stretched by the piling-up despair brought on by almost a decade of Reagan/Bush horrors. Stretched by a chaotic inner landscape that brought me a major dose of fear of flying.

In response to all this I feel lucky that I was also being stretched in a much more positive way by other surrounding forces. Stretched by an emerging culture of diversity in America in reaction to the racism of the Reagan administration. Stretched by my paralyzing air-travel phobia to sit myself down next to some human beings on a train in the middle of the night in Texas. Stretched to direct-action political activism by the carnage of the AIDS crisis. Stretched to imagine that one of art's chief functions is to foster change. As I say in the bratty, high-octane art/politics manifesto section of *Stretch Marks* where I re-stage a performance I did at a political demonstration for an AIDS ward in front of County General Hospital in Los Angeles:

> BECAUSE . . . maybe any function of art that does not basi-
> cally work in some kind of direction toward healing the sick
> . . . fostering communication . . . easing suffering . . . feeding
> bodies . . . or saving the planet just ought to get back to an
> apolitical, conceptual 1980 where it would be much more
> comfortable!!!

Stretch Marks is where I begin to find a political praxis, a way of telling my stories—in theaters, on the streets, in the pulpit, and in a jail—that created a bunch of highly engaged conversations with the world. The chaos continues of friends dying of AIDS, planes crashing, heroes being assassinated, hometowns having earthquakes, right-wing cabals becoming ascendant—but a way of responding as an artist and a citizen has started to make itself clear to me. I can't overestimate how transformed I was by two huge events in my life: my direct activism around AIDS with ACT UP and the explosion of new discourses that the multicultural revolution engendered. Suddenly as an artist I was getting to participate extensively in situations that shattered conventional theatrical performance—including creating guerrilla performance pieces for mass protest and civil disobedience actions with ACT UP—which rewired my connections between art and society.

At Macondo Espacio Cultural, a Salvadoran cultural center in Los Angeles, I collaborated with performers Guillermo Gómez-Peña, Rubén Martinez, Elia Arce, and others to create a work exploring bicultural dialogue and conflict.

I began teaching gay men's performance art workshops where we created exactly the rituals and performances that our tribe needed. These workshops provided a place for queer men to physically explore in full-color real time their most intimate narratives, memories, dreams, and possibilities with one another. Not only did these workshops allow me to understand in a grassroots way just what it means to be a community-based artist, they also were the springboard for hundreds of new artistic voices and several gay men's performance collectives that kept working together for years.

My regular collaborations with Reverend Malcolm Boyd in our controversial "performance art sermons" as part of the mass at St. Augustine by-the-Sea Episcopal Church in Santa Monica did more than stir the waters between the church and contemporary performance. We also got the biggest houses other than at Easter and Christmas Eve masses!

The ricochet of all these forces came together in 1989 when Linda Frye Burnham and I opened a new arts center, Highways Performance Space in Santa Monica, dedicated to providing a venue for diverse creative voices exploring the vortex of art, community, and social change. *Stretch Marks* would premiere at Highways three months after the space opened. Highways would be our clubhouse, our social club, our playpen, our Maoist self-critique slow-roasting barbecue, and a stage for thousands of performances and other interventions.

The cultural surf was definitely up! All of these experiences went right into the creation of *Stretch Marks*. A piece I performed at an ACT UP demo ended up in the performance. The whole structure of the performance is built around a mysterious and evocative train journey that is a metaphoric glue for the themes. A bittersweet tale of "cultural stretch" in the show comes directly from a life narrative about learning German from a Mexican lesbian named Fräulein Rodriguez that I dredged up for that wild night at Macondo. The whole show is suffused with the spiritual, dare I say shamanic, voice that my gay men's workshops and my collaborations as a parish performance artist were giving me. Finally *Stretch Marks* is haunted, penetrated even, by the overwhelming loss that filled that time whether from AIDS or exploded jet planes crashing at Lockerbie, Scotland. The performance is overflowing with a desire to find my place in history, to know where I come from culturally, and to feel an exchange with other human beings, an exchange as elusive yet tangible as the audience's flickering flashlights that illuminate the end of *Stretch Marks*.

All of these energies pushed, pulled, and stretched me toward a new kind of cultural practice, a new way of claiming voice and agency in the world, a new way of understanding the roles I can play (pun intended!) as an artist, a gay man, and a citizen.

(Tim enters in the dark carrying a birthday cake with thirty lit candles and a vintage Ken doll stuck in the middle of the frosting. With his beach bag over his shoulder, Tim drops a small trail of sand from his hand at the downstage edge of the performing area. The adagietto from Mahler's Fifth screeches off the record player and is replaced by a loud train.)

I am here. I am here on the beach. I'm here by the ocean. I'm waiting for a train to come here on the beach, here on Venice Beach. I'm on Speedo Lido. That's the homo one. I'll take any train that comes along. I swear I'm not picky. I'll take the *Desert Wind*, the *Trans-Siberian*, the *Southwest Chief*, the *Orient Express*, or the *Sunset Limited*.

I want these trains to come pounding down the sand or out from the horizon or down the boardwalk. This will be the express service from Avalon (and I don't mean Catalina). I mean Avalon, where King Arthur went and from where someday he will return. . . .

I am waiting here, watching the planes take off from Los Angeles International Airport, here by the salty edge of the ocean in Venice. But it's not just any ocean . . .

(Tim shakes his head till spit flys from his mouth—just to prove a point—and to get some of his salty saliva on the audience.)

. . . it's the Pacific Ocean.

People are blabbing a great deal about the Pacific Ocean— the Pacific Rim, the islands, the twenty-first century. The Pacific Ocean is not just a big blue spot on the globe or a buzzword for a trendoid cultural reference . . .

(Tim moves toward the audience and speaks to individuals.)

. . . the Pacific Ocean is where my life has taken place. The most intense moments: where I learned to swim, where I kissed my first boy on a church outing, where my family was happiest together, where I took acid on the winter solstice and lay for hours in the seaweed at low tide. It is the ocean where my father is buried, a few miles out that way. It's where I will be buried too, I suppose, unless there is a nuclear war or I get lined up against a wall and shot and bulldozed into a mass grave. Or we get the big oceany-earthquake experience, which is picturesquely called liquefaction. Now, liquefaction is not a new and satisfying milk shake at 7-Eleven. Liquefaction is what the experts think will happen to all the low-lying silty areas like Venice Beach if (or when) a big earthquake happens. Basically the dirt will turn to liquid, kind of like quicksand, and drop a few hundred feet, and the ocean will pour right down my street, Venice Boulevard, and head straight for my driveway covering up me, my garden, my boyfriend, and my dog.

But in the meantime, I walk and swim almost every day along Santa Monica Bay. Here at my beach in Venice.

(Tim goes upstage and pins California towel and other beach stuff he pulls from his bag to the up left wall.)

I love the beach. Everyone comes here and takes off a lot of their clothes and their preconceptions and their jobs and lays down and offers their bodies to the ocean. They create a little world around their towels: the chair, the book, the bag full of refreshing beverages. Then they sit next to lots of other almost naked mammals here on the beach.

(Tim strikes beach tableau comical pose.)

At my beach, here on the cusp of Speedo Lido, everyone has their way of getting into the ocean.

Some people dip one toe in. Some people walk briskly in then see it's cold and walk briskly out. Some people (certain hirsute fellows, generally) run mad-dog style into the surf, leaving foam in their wake. A delicious photo opportunity, that.

There are all kinds of people: older polar bear types, Salvadoran families, folks from Watts, German tourists, gay boys (of which I am a variety) with their triple-D pecs and swimsuits tucked into the crack of their ass so they can tan their butts.

Everybody laid out offering their bodies in nice rows to the ocean. It's a lot like the supermarket . . . or a train ride . . . or death. . . .

(Tim does gesture sequence . . . towel shake . . . sand brush . . . head shake.)

I guess. Everyone stripped, completely the same and completely different.

There are strong handsome men and women in red bathing suits here, lifeguards they are called. They're ready to intervene if the stakes get too high, the breathing too fast, the flesh too tired. Then they jump in and save you. It's an excellent arrangement. Everyone watches them. From the leggy run through the shallows . . . to the shouldery swim . . . to the meeting amid the riptide . . . to the return. The savee always a little sheepish but still grateful. And then the order returns. Heads go back under hats.

People return to their towels . . . a little ripple . . . a tiny gamble . . . nothing to write home about . . . no gory details at 11:00. Because there are lifeguards here.

(Tim does gestures and crossses downstage close to audience.)

But I have found myself from time to time at a place where there are no lifeguards, a place called Zero Beach. This is a place where Rod Serling puts on his baggies and anything might happen. For a while I thought for sure that Zero Beach was in Far Rockaway at the Beach 67th/Gaston Ave stop on the A Train. There is nothing there but burnt-out buildings, a frayed boardwalk, torn-up hard-core sex magazines blowing in the wind over broken glass. I was sure this was Zero Beach. And so it was once. I was there on my twenty-first birthday and a young black girl drowned there on the rocks. That was her Zero Beach.

And now everywhere has become Zero Beach. Here in Venice, the ground zero of my life . . . bull's-eye . . . corn hole. I am here with Gustave von Aschenbach from *Death in Venice* and Maria von Trapp from *The Sound of Music.* I am their love child. Together we sit watching the airplanes take off from LAX, watching the cute boys jog, watching Zero Beach.

I wear my father's dog tag from World War II. The dog tag he carried across the Pacific when he was seventeen. I have it around my neck now. There is a cute German boy on my right and a cute Japanese boy on my left. Then there's me with my father's dog tag, the only trophy I have of the twentieth century, right here in the middle. My feet in the wet sand . . . my head under a wave . . . the water which reaches to the Americas . . . and to Asia . . . and to the Star-Kist tuna cannery in Terminal Island, too . . . Terminal Island . . . next to Zero Beach.

I am waiting for a train. I check the schedule. It's due any minute now or maybe in fifty years. I watch the planes taking off from LAX. I wonder which one of them will explode.

I wait some more.

(Tim makes his hand into an airplane as the lights go dark. The sound of jackhammers fades up. He stomps and flies cross stage. Tim straps on the huge airplane costume and takes his position for take-off. The sad bit from Beethoven's Seventh haunts the runway.)

Once upon a time . . .
I was a Prince of Flight . . .
A Captain of Soaring . . .
Intimate of Updrafts . . .
Master of Gravity . . .
Lord of Cloud . . . Wind . . . and the very Ozone Layer itself!!!
Since childhood I had rushed headlong in my pursuit of flight—I experimented with umbrellas, flammable lighter-than-air gases, cut-out plywood wings on my arms off windy promontories—whatever it would take to shake the earth from my impatient and ambitious feet. As a kid I savored dirigibles, studied gliders, stroked the smooth fuselage of prop planes. I never met a Cessna I didn't like!

I threw myself out of airplanes. Pulled the rip cord in ecstasy. Hang-glided from high New England beachy cliffs. I was always happy in the air in my window seat in front of the wing on the Boeing 727, my breath fogging the glass that reflected my face . . .

But now, something has happened. Flight has left me. The skies aren't so friendly anymore. I don't care if they do it best—I'm not ready for Delta anymore, and the sight of a passenger plane sets me shivering.

I who once floated happily thousands of feet above the earth dangling beneath parachutes!

I who once swooped through the air cradled under a human-size kite am now terrified to fly to Columbus, Ohio, or over the Columbia River, and certainly not down to Colombia!

Not on your life!!! Not on a bet!!!

And definitely not on an airplane!!!

And now when I have to fly, and often I must, I follow my special ritual. I take out a lot of travel insurance. I have my friend Dona, who's a witch, light magical, blue, travel-candles. I prepare a special calming cocktail—Stolichnaya and codeine with a Xanax chaser—that I guzzle pre-flight. I put my affairs in order, tidy up my desk. I don special travel underwear, bleached their whitest white, purified garments for the flight to 37,000 feet. I get a seat near an exit in the back. Or is it better to be near the front? Oh shit I can't remember. I fly only on very large, seemingly dependable airplanes, preferably 747's with their names painted on the side. Names like *Pride of Denver* or *Spirit of Flight*. I prefer airlines from obsessive and technologically anal countries, like Japan Airlines or Lufthansa, but United might do in a pinch ... in a pinch ... in a pinch. . . .

Somebody pinch me I must be dreaming!!! This big fat airplane full of unsavory Americans in polyester jumpsuits can't possibly take off and then safely arrive at Newark airport. It must be a joke! But here we are jockeying for position on the runway. There is no doubt in my mind that this plane will explode a few moments after we become airborne and then will smash into an overpass on the San Diego Freeway decapitating a mother of eight in a Volvo. . . .

We're next for takeoff. Why does everyone seem so cheerful? Don't they know we're about to share a horrific and collective death? This will be a mass of pissing shitting puking fear-filled protoplasm to be fried over-easy into huevos-gross-out-rancheros!!!!

The engines begin to race. We are rolling faster and faster down the runway. I am thrown back into my seat. I grip the seat handles. This is it I guess. I say prayers to every world religion I can think of. I make shameless promises that if I get out of this I will be more appreciative of things. I will love and honor them!!!

I love my boyfriend. I love my 1974 Gremlin. I love the letters of Thomas Mann. I love blow jobs. I love cups of coffee. And now I'm going to have to leave all of that!!!

Give up all the pleasures and pride of the zillion thrills and chills that flesh is heir to.

(Beethoven music collides with Peter Pan "I'm Flying" and reaches ear-splitting volume.)

Father, I have flown too high. The sun has melted the wax on my wings.

Father, I'm falling into the sea.

I'm falling!

FAAAAAAAAAAAAAAATHEEEEEEEEEEEEEEE-RRRRRRRRRRRRRRRRRRRRRR!!!!!

(The anvil chorus from Il Trovatore *begins as fear of fly-ing litany peaks. Tim hangs up cut-out travel images on the clothesline—a locomotive, the* Titanic, *a bomb, a jet plane—and gets out of airplane costume. Tim approaches the cake doing a slashing knife dance as "Climb Every Mountain" from* The Sound of Music *very slowly plays. Tim blows out candles.)*

I have always been obsessed by travel disaster.

The *Titanic* slipping beneath the icy waves as an ultimate and convenient symbol for an end of an era, the limits of tech-nology. . . .

The *Hindenburg* exploding in the sky over New Jersey, con-suming itself in thirty-seven seconds. The swastikas on its tail the last thing to burn as they peeled and crackled off like the wrap-per on a Three Musketeers candy bar.

I would stare at these pictures like they were sex and more . . . alpha and omega . . . *Götterdämmerung* and morning in America.

It seemed like these travel disasters meant that somebody was demanding a sacrifice to appease the old gods. It was time for the technological big boys on the block to pay up for their misdeeds. These sinking, crashing, and exploding things were the tasty Technicolor metaphor for a world about to eat its own tail.

I would look at these pictures in my big travel-disaster picture book when I was ten or eleven. Watch movies on TV about ships sinking and nights to remember. Cry when George C. Scott fails to defuse the bomb that blows up the zeppelin. I would press my ten- or eleven-year-old hard-on into the heavy-pile, emerald-green shag carpet as I flipped the pages of my big travel disaster book and then I would go out and play. I was happy, so happy, that that would never happen to meeeeeeeeeeeeeeeee!!!!!

(Tim drops face in birthday cake. What a mess.)

But now, metaphor becomes reality.
Morning becomes electrical wing-flap failure.
And misery is the 1:15 flight to San Jose.
Which is why I take the train.

(Tim picks up suitcase, does wild train dance, goes into audience and pulls a basin of water out from under a seat. Tim gives it to an audience member and has them help him wash the cake off his face.)

I took the train for eight thousand miles this fall. From Union Station, LA, to New Orleans on the *Sunset Limited*. New Orleans to Atlanta on the *Crescent*. Atlanta to NYC also on the *Crescent*. NYC to Toronto on the *Maple Leaf*. Toronto to Chicago on the *Lakeshore Limited*. From Chicago back home to LA on the *Southwest Chief*!

The train is a funny place. It's a place where you might actually sit next to and talk to people who aren't at all like yourself. It's an odd bunch that take the train: old people, the Amish, people afraid to fly, European tourists, poor people on their ninety-nine-dollar unlimited tickets, and me. There is a weird intimacy that exists—especially on a long trip. It takes fifty-one hours from LA to New Orleans. There's no stewardess to tell you where to sit. There's no in-flight movie that makes you slip down the plastic and shut out the light. This is no quickie, alienated postmodern

hip hop from point LA to point NYC. Nope. You have to look at things. You have to watch the time and endless miles go by. You have to actually see Kansas . . . become Colorado become New Mexico become Arizona become the Mojave Desert become here.

And when you walk into a crowded dining car and sit down at a table with a bunch of strangers the question you most often hear is, "Where ya headin'?" Seems like a simple question, but what that question really means and how it is sometimes heard is, "What is the meaning of life and why are you on this train?"

When that question is asked you better be ready to ante up. Otherwise get your cherry pie to go and get out of the game. This is the main reason I like taking the train. There is a disarming candor about it. No appearances to keep up. No telephones to answer. No errands to run. There's a rock and a rumble and a sway that I like. It's like being asleep in the back of the station wagon late at night when your parents drive you home from your horrible aunt and uncle in West Covina.

The rock. The rumble. The sway.

I went with my boyfriend Doug to Union Station to leave on my six-week eight-thousand-mile trip. We got there and checked my baggage . . .

(Tim flings his suitcase through the air.)

. . . and waited in that big Spanish deco hall. This was going to be the longest we had ever been apart. Doug and I had said good-bye in many places—airports, the subway, bus terminals, through the open window of an automobile, even once parting in anger in the cold gray drizzle of the Parc Royal in Brussels—but this was different. Bigger, but smaller, too. More like a campfire than a microwave, more permanent somehow, like once the slow growl of a locomotive gets moving it might be very hard and take a long time to get back.

I had entered a whole other layer of experience there at Union Station in downtown LA, a whole other world where wood and steel connects you in a line with where you are going to go.

I got on the train and put my stuff in my sleeping compartment. The little bed was all laid out, a small bottle of bad wine waiting for me on the stiff starched pillowcase. There was a place for all my things—a shelf for my book, Thomas Wolfe's *Of Time and the River*, a nook for my glasses, a hiding spot for my porn magazines between the mattress and armrest.

I came back down onto the platform and Doug and I hugged and kissed as the diesel horn blew and shook us to our tennis shoes. The nice woman conductor told us it was time to go. I climbed back on the train and she shut the door. The train rocked forward imperceptibly and then back. And then forward. I pressed my face to the glass as Doug walked along with the train as it slowly began to leave Union Station. This was so intimate and close to the bone. The two of us there—one on a train beginning to move and the other still on the platform. Which one of us was moving and which was standing still? As the train moved quicker so did Doug until he was walking as fast as he could alongside. Then he was running faster and faster until he couldn't keep up anymore. Finally he was just a little waving curly-headed speck there at the end of Platform 6, Union Station, LA. The train picked up speed and went over the river and I couldn't see him anymore.

I am on the train moving through my life and the history of the world. . . .

I LOOKED LEFT and I saw my long-dead grandparents' house there on the train tracks by Mission Road in Alhambra and the very same tracks where as a kid I put pennies and nickels to be squashed under the Union Pacific. . . .

I LOOKED RIGHT and I see the deer of the fields of Marienborn as my train heads through East Germany on my way to Berlin. I am twenty-seven. Those deer are playing around in the grass there in the no-man's-land between the war and what was next to come. . . .

I LOOK UP and I'm standing between the cars on the IRT subway in New York. I am heading downtown on my way home from a friend's AIDS memorial and I scream up at the damp roof of the subway tunnel!

I LOOK DOWN and I see a scarred and sooty ten-pence coin there on the tracks as my train comes into Victoria Station as I arrive in London for the first time.

I am on a red trolley heading toward Tijuana!

I am on the sealed train that brought Lenin to Saint Petersburg!

I am on the funeral train taking Lincoln's body home to Springfield!

I am on the *Twentieth-Century Limited* bringing the Dodgers to LA!

I am on the train that brought Phyllis Diller to Hollywood!

The Jews to Auschwitz!

The tourists to Tomorrowland!

THE TROLLEY TO TIJUANA!!!!!!!

We are pulling into a station. What does the sign say? BERLIN-BAHNHOFZOO! I have left Union Station and traveled all the way across the country underneath the Atlantic Ocean through Europe and now here we are in Berlin!!! There's a large crowd of people here to greet me. They carry big signs that say WILLKOMMEN! The Adorable Jewish Boyfriend Douglas is there wearing a prayer shawl and is getting ready to sing his favorite Oktoberfest song. Didn't I just leave him at Union Station? I better get ready. What should I wear when getting off in Berlin in 1931?

(Tim opens suitcase. Puts on sailor hat. Nope, throws it back in. Then puts on lederhosen instead.)

I just happen to have my lederhosen here. What luck! As I slip into them I hear a cumbia by Sonora Dynamita play over the station loudspeakers. It's a cumbia about AIDS. An announcement over a loudspeaker says this train is leaving for Guadalajara!!!

I better hurry. I'm struggling to get into these fucking lederhosen—just one more antler button. Slap on my Alpine hat and I
grab my suitcase. I rush out of my compartment down the hall
out onto the platform . . . and there's no one there.

The train is gone. I'm standing in my lederhosen at the abandoned train station in Whittier, California. The wind is blowing.
All I can hear is some yodeling in the distance and the rock and
clang of a disappearing freight train. Welcome to Whittier.

*(Tim has scrambled into his lederhosen and alpine hat,
done his fake German Schubladen slapping dance and
stands poised at the edge of cultural stretch.)*

I grew up here in Whittier, California. On Whittier Boulevard at Pounds Avenue. To get to Whittier you go from downtown LA over the Sixth Street bridge through the barrio underneath the arch that says "Welcome to Whittier Boulevard,"
Champs Elysées of East LA. Through Montebello. Past Pico
Rivera. Over the San Gabriel River to Whittier!

I learned German here from a Chicana lesbian named
Fräulein Rodriguez. I am not sure what twist of fate brought me
here to study German with Fräulein Rodriguez, but I know that
it happened. I think somehow I got mixed up when I changed
trains in Mexicali to get on the connecting service through Sri
Lanka for Hamburg and that I ended up here on the abandoned
train station in Whittier wearing my lederhosen. It is very strange.
I am ready to learn from Fräulein Rodriguez the irregular forms
of the verb "to be."

Ich bin. Ich war. Ich werde sein!

It is 1972 in Whittier. Which at that time, when I was about
to learn the irregular forms of the verb "to be" from Fräulein
Rodriguez, had not yet been destroyed by an earthquake. Which
at that time had a big sign which said WELCOME TO WHIT-
TIER—HOMETOWN OF PRESIDENT RICHARD NIXON.
Which at that time was sometimes called WHITE-ier.

Ich bin. Ich war. Ich werde sein!

I grew up hearing a weird Spanish in our house. No, we didn't have Spanish-speaking maids or anything. This was hard-core, middle-class, middle-brow, San Gabriel Valley peasant routine, okay? Both my parents sold things. My mom on the floor at May Company department store and my dad as a traveling salesman. He was really into speaking Spanish. When he came back from World War II he taught himself from a book called *El español al dia*.

I grew up hearing and saying things like . . .

"Pass the mantequilla."

"Can I have some more leche, por favor?"

"Honey, please get me a cerveza!"

I was called Timoteo, which is a name I don't think anyone in Latin America even has! At the end of every perfect California day, my mom would tuck me in and say, "Hasta la mañana, Timoteo."

Which was the only Spanish I ever learned until this year.

I grew up on Whittier Boulevard. Not far from my house, just over the San Gabriel River, was the mansion of Pio Pico, the last (so far anyway) Mexican governor of California. This always confused me as a little kid. What was the house of the last (so far anyway) Mexican governor of California doing at the corner of Whittier and Pioneer Boulevards just across the street from Vons supermarket? Where did Pio Pico go? Did he still live there? What's going on? Did he go back to Mexico in 1847? Did they kill him? Imprison him? They named a boulevard for him. What ever happened to Pio Pico?

To learn the answer to this and other questions, in 1972, the same year I began learning the irregular forms of the verb "to be" from Fräulein Rodriguez, I also took a summer school course called California Heritage.

(Tim runs to beach towel and points to mission locations.)

We learned more than anyone should ever have to know about the state of California. We learned about the horrors of the conquistadores. The bravery of Sir Francis Drake and the *Golden Hind* sailing into San Francisco Bay. The wet foot of Cabrillo as he claimed California for Spain at Point Loma in San Diego. We would go on endless field trips to all the missions. I would write and perform little plays about Father Junipero Serra. These plays had titles like "In Which Father Serra Whips Father Jose!" or "In Which Father Serra Brutally and Unremittingly Scourges the Recalcitrant Indigenous People." We visited some battlefield near San Diego where our teacher whose name was (I am not kidding) Mr. West, said, "Okay kids, everybody off the bus to see where U.S. imperialism stole California from Mexico!!!"

We smoked dope in the tannery of Mission La Purissima de Santa Inez in Lompoc. I stole a hunk of adobe as a souvenir from Mission San Gabriel by my grandma's house. I pined away for the adorable Roger Blaney in the cool mystery of the chapel at Mission San Juan Capistrano, which is widely known as the "Queen of the Missions."

The next year my sister Betsy married Jorge Olmedo and our whole family life changed. Suddenly Jorge and his huge Cuban extended family became the center of our world in Whittier. Christmas dinner became black beans and yucca, not ham and cranberry sauce. Under the influence of Cuban warmth, my family started getting huggy with everybody. Jorge's mom and dad were pretty old and didn't speak much English, so this was my dad's big chance. Out came *El español al dia* and my dad was speaking Spanish. My sister was speaking Spanish. My brother Greg, fresh from a year in Lima with his Peruvian girlfriend Jezebel, was speaking really good Spanish. It was at this point that I began my study of German with Fräulein Rodriguez.

I don't know why I picked German. It didn't really make sense. It had no relation to reality. It just meant that I couldn't talk to Jorge's parents on Sundays. It was like I was refusing to be where I actually was: in Whittier, California, with an enormous Cuban extended family in the late twentieth century! Clearly I should have been taking Spanish in second period with Señorita Rodriguez and not German in fifth with Fräulein Rodriguez! My study of German made sense, in that I am German. German/English. German/Scotch. German/Flemish. German/Alsatian! German/Scotch! Scotch and Water. The water underneath my feet, reaching to the Americas and Asia and to the Star-Kist tuna cannery in Long Beach, too. . . .

(Hypnotized by this steamy, simmering melting pot, Tim slaps himself to snap out of it.)

Let's just say, I got *very* into my German study.

I would read Schiller in the original as I ate my Cap'n Crunch every morning. I forced my family to begin observing Oktoberfest as religiously as we did Christmas. I made them dress up in traditional lederhosen and dirndl to go to Alpine Village, the German cultural theme and amusement park right off the San Diego Freeway in Torrance. I subscribed to and religiously read the Los Angeles German-language newspaper, the *California Staats-Zeitung*. At a certain point I got a little too into it with a group of friends after seeing *A Clockwork Orange* at the Egyptian Theater on Hollywood Boulevard when we gathered around a piano in our proto-punk attire and sang "Deutschland, Deutschland über Alles."

It was hard for us white kids to know who we actually were as we dog-paddled desperately through the blankness of a suburban childhood. You just tried to grab onto *something*, lasso a kind of identity life preserver, and hope you didn't drown. This is probably why I studied German.

Fräulein Rodriguez was a very good, but widely feared teacher. She was also the advisor for the MECHA group at my high school, the Chicano kids' cultural and political club. I could have been taking Spanish with her too, but I didn't. That's too bad, because though she was a very good German teacher, I bet she was ace at Spanish. Fräulein Rodriguez mostly hung out with another lesbian teacher at our high school, Miss Schneider, a very strict biology instructor. Miss Schneider looked just like Ernest Borgnine in *McHale's Navy*. Fräulein Rodriguez and Miss Schneider would walk down the hallways together lost in conversation. Some high school kids, being the complete creeps that they usually are, made fun of them a lot behind their backs. "Look out! Here comes the faculty lesbian and gay parade!" Once or twice I even shouted this out too, which was quite a joke since I was just about to bloom into the biggest fag at my high school.

Fräulein Rodriguez and I had a complicated relationship. She was a real authoritarian and would drill us ruthlessly in our conjugations, declensions, and adjective endings. Fräulein Rodriguez and I would fight a lot in class about stuff, argue about issues of *Realpolitik*. We had to get along though. I was, after all, the best German student at school. In fact, eventually in my senior year I was the only German 4 student at my high school doing independent study. This is when I really began to learn the irregular forms of the verb "to be."

Ich bin. Ich war. Ich werde sein!

In 1975, at the beginning of my senior year, I finally completely figured out that I liked boys. I began to manifest my newly discovered sexual identity in the behaviors of my era. Black nail polish, black lipstick, black eyeliner. This neo-goth look is still very popular across our troubled land. Occasionally I would add a special fashion accent, a black velour floor-length cape, but only on pep rally days. I showed everyone the class ring my boyfriend from a rival high school had given me. I also began making up the most outlandish fantasy narratives of all the sex I imagined I was having on the mean streets of Hollywood. My best girlfriend Kim Bertola was so impressed with my stories she became my personal homosexuality PR agent. Kim wrote on every available surface at my high school—desk tops, lockers—TIM GIVES GOOD HEAD. She was such a good friend she even went to the stencil T-shirt shop at the mall and made me a T-shirt with that message! I would wear this shirt to my high school every other Wednesday, and if anyone so much as looked at me sideways I would freeze them with my homo death glare!

Fräulein Rodriguez noticed these things. But she said nothing. For my independent study course with Fräulein Rodriguez, I was translating Thomas Mann's *Death in Venice* from German to English. This was not easy. Often Fräulein Rodriguez and I would sit together late after school. The two of us leaning over the page, an Anglo-Germano homo and a Latina lesbian untangling the pleasures of the subjunctive case *auf Deutsch*.

I shared my progress on a tricky part of my translation with Fräulein Rodriguez one afternoon. I had gotten to the point in *Death in Venice* where Gustave von Aschenbach, this uptight-closet-case-writer-from-Munich, has gone to Venice on a package vacation. He quickly falls in love with the beautiful Polish jailbait boy named Tadzio with bad big seventies hair. Gustave follows Tadzio around, making the boy's mother very nervous. Finally he gets lost following them in the back alleys of Venice and he collapses into a heap on the plague-strewn piazza and whispers a confession to his deepest place of psychic self. "I love you, Tadzio!"

When I got to that point in my translation, I sort of flipped out. I didn't cry hysterically or anything. I am, after all, a WASP. But my lower lip did quiver noticeably. Who did I think I was? Gustave von Aschenbach or a teenage queer boy with bad makeup? The truth was I didn't give good head. I'd never given anyone head! I wasn't even exactly sure what *head* even was!

Fräulein Rodriguez looked at me quietly and shut her copy of *Death in Venice*. She said, pointing at my Halloween midnight black nail polish, "*Das ist nicht nötig*. That isn't necessary. *Sei stolz!* Be proud of yourself. *Alles stimmt*. It's okay." Fräulein Rodriguez placed her hand on my shoulder but she said nothing, for she was a Chicana lesbian of few words. Then she quickly picked up the book and we went back to our translation. At that exact moment the entire Lowell High School varsity water polo team loudly walked past the open classroom door after their practice. I could smell the chlorine on their skin rising from their bodies, chlorine from the pool full of men I was about to dive into. I was getting ready to move on. I was going to get out of high school soon. I looked forward to the moment at graduation when the entire Lowell High School chorus would sing some maudlin and inspiring song from a Rodgers and Hammerstein musical as I clutched my diploma. I would get older, a tiny bit wiser, maybe even reach the ripe old age of thirty! Who knows? Eventually I might even learn how to give good head! Then I would think of Fräulein Rodriguez and how she always hoped I would someday study Spanish too but I never did until this year. I have my father's book, *El español al dia*, *"y finalmente estudio español."* I think of Fräulein Rodriguez and thank her for teaching me the most important thing, the irregular forms of the verb "to be." I am. I was. I will be.

Danke schön, Fräulein Rodriguez.

(Tim puts on his alpine hat and as the lights fade he stamps out the years from eighteen to thirty. With each pound of his feet the lights flash in the audience's eyes.)

Since then, I have been stretched, and pulled, and mashed, and squished . . . by this unkind century.

EXHIBIT A! Gray hair!

EXHIBIT B! Scar from carved out blood tumor!

EXHIBIT C! Skin graft from here to here. Cut off end of finger on the day the Pope was shot!

EXHIBIT D! Faint, but visible, stretch marks back here in the butt zone. Testament to the ceaseless bend and sway of life.

EXHIBIT E! Parts of my heart torn out by the early loss of friends, lovers, and family.

I am used merchandise.

A 1958 model.

There is a mountain out by where the trains come over Cajon Pass coming into LA. In beautiful Colton, near San Bernardino.

I've been watching this mountain a long time, for my whole life. They've been slowly tearing this mountain down. . . .

Rock by rock.

Scoop by scoop.

Foot by foot.

It must be made out of something useful, something valuable. Like bauxite . . . or Oil of Olay.

It used to be a very high mountain. And now it's only half of what it was.

And it's probably been turned into Ziploc bags, jet engines, and railroad tracks. . . .

(Pounding pile driver sounds fill the space.)

CHOP. GRATE. GRIND. STIR. PUREE. WHIP. MIX. BLEND. LIQUEFY. FRAPPE.

Let's face it, any way you slice or dice it, we are all used merchandise. Like me. Like that mountain. I turned thirty this year.

(The Broadway recording of "Climb Every Mountain" comes on. Every show needs a musical number! Tim speaks the text along with that fabulous nun singing the lyrics.)

CLIMB EVERY MOUNTAIN	I had a birthday party last year. It was my birthday party. My twenty-ninth birthday.
SEARCH HIGH AND LOW	I had eaten too much sushi. Drunk too many sloe gin fizzes.
FOLLOW EVERY BYWAY	I became sick to my stomach. Soon I would throw up . . .
EVERY PATH YOU KNOW	And I knew I would be seeing those twelve California rolls and that bowl of creamed corn once again.

CLIMB EVERY MOUNTAIN	So I decided to rush home. So that I could puke in private.
FORD EVERY STREAM	When I got home. I turned on the TV and waited.
FOLLOW EVERY RAINBOW	There was a movie on KTLA channel 5. There were all these nuns looking holy and humming.
TILL YOU FIND YOUR DREAM	Wait a minute! I know these nuns. I know this movie! This musical! It's one of my favorite things!
A DREAM THAT WILL NEED	It's at the point in the movie where the one young nun has given up on life . . .
ALL THE LOVE YOU CAN GIVE	She has quit, returned to the convent, and then the head honcho nun tells her she has to go back into the world and fight for her dreams!
EVERY DAY OF YOUR LIFE	And suddenly I'm at my graduation from high school When the Lowell High School chorus sang this song. It turned my stomach then too!!
FOR AS LONG AS YOU LIVE	It told me that I was supposed to move upward and on to forge things in the smithy of my soul to strive and not to yield!!!

CLIMB EVERY MOUNTAIN	As the nun's singing was about to peak I knew it was time! I was going to have those nuns help me climb my way to the bathroom!!
FORD EVERY STREAM	I got up from my sickbed and took a step. I covered my mouth. I didn't want to toss up in my typewriter!
FOLLOW EVERY RAINBOW	I saw a harsh glow at the end of the hall, a glow on the toilet bowl. Just one more step! One more step!

(A gleaming white toilet seat flies in from the heavens. A toilet ex machina!)

TILL YOU FIND YOUR DREAM	I made it! I fall to my knees. My chin on the rim. My face reflected in those still toilet bowl waters. The smell of Sani-Flush wafting over my entire body!
A DREAM THAT WILL NEED	I embraced that cool indifferent toilet bowl and I said a little prayer. "Oh please God, no sharp chunks or burning acids!"
ALL THE LOVE YOU CAN GIVE	I saw the world with different eyes. That toilet scum line my only horizon.

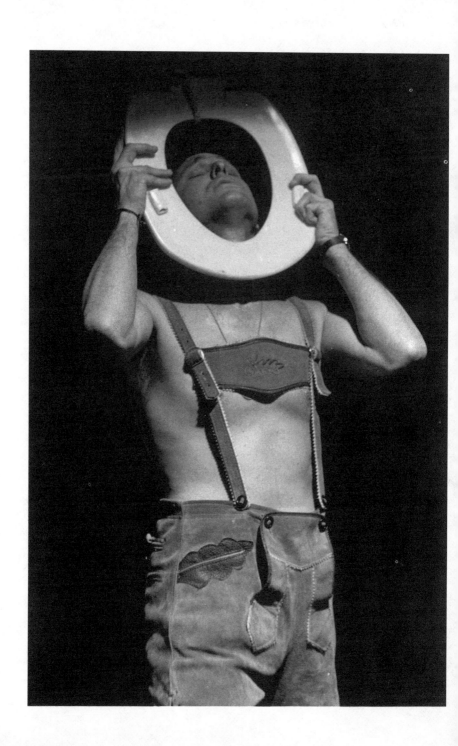

EVERY DAY OF YOU LIFE

I wanted to tell that singing nun
that things aren't always that great.
Students are being massacred!
People are dying of AIDS!!!

FOR AS LONG AS YOU LIVE

It's not just a day-hike from birthday
to birthday.
And this was a lesson I was going to
learn on a gut level.
For now it was BARF-O-RAMA
time!

CLIMB EVERY MOUNTAIN

It just came up.
It was like turning on a switch of a
garbage disposal—
up it came!

(Tim barfs.)

FORD EVERY STREAM

I just wanna stick around!
Acting-Up as much as I can.
It's my party and I'll puke
if I want to.

(Barf.)

FOLLOW EVERY RAINBOW

I wanna live to puke again!
I WANNA LIVE TO PUKE
AGAIN!!!

(Barf.)

TILL YOU FIND YOUR DREAM

THAT'S *(barf)* WHAT *(barf)*
LIFE'S *(barf)* ABOUT!!!!

*(The toilet flies back up to the ceiling and Tim begins doing
deep knee bends, counting from his age projecting into the sev-*

*enties. Then Tim makes a big stomp coming out of the birth-
day count. The lights flash.)*

We're here.

We're here by the ocean.

We're here in Colton, California, where the freight train derails and wipes out a whole suburban neighborhood.

We're here in Colton a week later when the gas line ruptured by the derailed freight train explodes and wipes out a whole other suburban neighborhood.

We're here in Beijing, in Tiananmen Square with the student doing the pas de deux with the tank.

1 and 2 and 1 and 2. . . .

We're here in the stadium at Santiago de Chile where my friend Roberto's brother is about to get his dick cut off during his torture-murder by the fascist General Pinochet.

We're here now in the wrong row on Flight 232. Oops!

We're here with poor Alyosha Karamazov, of course, being offered unfair ironies about tortures by Turks.

We're here on the beach with Gustave von Aschenbach and Maria von Trapp who are about to have a love child and I am that child . . . ready to go out into the world.

We're here in front of County General Hospital in East LA.

*(Tim sets the scene in front of the hospital. Places his
props—a bag of sand and a knife—then sets the wooden
box that will be the stage.)*

County General is the biggest hospital in the world. Right here is a big mean iron fence. Over here are banners and signs. Symbols of protest. Manifestation. Over here—from this part of the audience over to here—there are tents. A community is living here on the pavement. From this person in the audience over to here are TV cameras. Reporters. Journalists. And up here are votive candles, hundreds and hundreds of votive candles. Okay, let's recap: Protest signs. Community. Media. Votive candles. The four basic food groups. This is the ACT UP–LA week-long vigil in front of County Hospital in January 1989. For a week we've been living here on the pavement to force the fucking County of LA to provide an AIDS ward here at the biggest hospital in the world. This is the closing rally. I have been asked, since I've been here most of the week, to make a performance for the closing rally. They have provided a performance space, which is very important to me. They have also provided a stage for me, which is somewhat less important. I have my props. Which are of utmost importance to me. People are doing speeches. Singing songs. It's my turn. I come out of the audience. Approach the stage and begin.

(Tim steps up on his soap box, stomps, and sings the following like in a mass.)

FOR THE AIDS COALITION TO UNLEASH POWER (ACT UP–LA) WEEK-LONG VIGIL IN FRONT OF COUNTY GENERAL HOSPITAL. WE'RE HERE TO DEMAND PROPER CARE, PROGRAMS, AND AN AIDS WARD HERE AT THE BIGGEST HOSPITAL IN THE WORLD!

There is a big building behind me—a very big building—and on this building these words are written: "Erected by the citizens of the County of Los Angeles to provide hospital care for the acutely ill and suffering to whom the doctors of the attending staff give their services without charge in order that no citizen of the County shall be deprived of health or life for lack of such care and services."

There is a big building behind me. I looked up at these words this morning after waking up on the cold cement and going to the bathroom by the perpetually blood-stained walls of the public toilet. Why do those words sound so old and crinkly? Like they just slithered off some asshole's Victrola? Have the county board

of supervisors, or the mayor, or the governor, or our brand-new, fucking President Bush ever read those words?!? Which were chiseled in during the administration of Herbert Hoover, THAT TACKY QUEEN!!!

OOPS, sorry Herb. I got you mixed up with your girlfriend, J. Edgar.

And lots of us have been gathered here this week to try to make those words become true.

(Tim stabs knife into a bag of sand he holds in one hand. It begins to pour out.)

As I sat on the beach on Inauguration Day, the day before this vigil began, I sat in Venice near the homo zone, a.k.a. Speedo Lido, and three things happened: I saw the jet airplanes taking off from LAX and I thought of my recent and brutal fear of flying and about Elizabeth Marek who died in the bombing of Flight 103 over Lockerbie, Scotland. She was from here, in Venice Beach, and was a spectacular lesbian and performer and peace activist who got blown up at 33,000 feet. No conclusions there, just a little context.

I watched the planes taking off over the Pacific Ocean and on the beach arrived a midwestern tourist family, shooting lots of pictures to be sent back to Hays, Kansas, with the caption "HERE WE ARE ON THE BEACH IN JANUARY!" This group included a mother type who shouts to the others very loud, "I DON'T CARE WHAT ANY OF YOU WANT. I HAVE NO INTEREST IN GOING TO MEXICO!"

And then I heard an announcement over the loudspeaker on the lifeguard's truck which says, "ATTENTION!!! ALL LIFEGUARDS! BEGIN CHECKING ALL PERSONS LAYING IN THE SUN TO SEE IF ANY OF THEM ARE A DEAD BODY!!!"

This is the world I am living in this day in front of County General Hospital.

There is a building. There is a big building. There is a big building on the hill behind me. Something has been happening here in front of this building. People have passed seven days and seven nights in front of this building together. Soup has been made. Stories have been told. Performances have been done. TV cameras have been pointed. Wet sloppy noisy sex has been had by those two persevering dudes in that pup tent over there, wobbling and shaking, and I say unto you now that if Boy Scouts had been like this I might have made it past Tenderfoot. Gestures have been made, sleeping on the pavement in the cold and the rain. Most intense of all we've seen what each other looks like before coffee in the morning and yet still we are here. Because demands have been made, demands to this city, county, state, and country to help our people live.

Now, what has actually happened here? Has all this stuff made County General Hospital rise from its foundations and fly away trailing its rotten plumbing, sadnesses, and a thousand IV tubes doing a slow anti-viral drip as it disappears over the barrio? No. That has not happened. But maybe it will make some other things happen. . . .

LIKE MAYBE . . . when the county gets its shit together . . . people who are dealing with AIDS stuff right now and don't have health insurance will have a place to go where they won't have to sit in a public hallway on a hard bench getting their chemo and throw up from the side-effects in view of all . . .

LIKE MAYBE . . . it will begin to seem to more of us . . . that it is at least as important to get people who need it proper health care ASAP as it is to shop for a new leather jacket or to make yet another performance piece which obliquely deconstructs print advertising . . . and believe me I've made my share of those . . .

LIKE MAYBE ... a new kind of community is being born ...

LIKE MAYBE ... sleeping outside here in East LA has stretched a few of us to think in a real way what it is like for the eighty thousand people who will sleep in cardboard boxes in this City of Angels tonight—some of whom have gathered here with us, walked the four miles from Skid Row, shared some food, and found a safer place to sleep through the night ...

LIKE MAYBE ... this is a whole new cultural time arriving ... of people gathered around a bunch of votive candles trying to tell each other a coupla stories waiting for the morning to come ...

LIKE MAYBE ... we fags and lesbos can become a model for how Americans can stop forgetting and holding in and avoiding and feeding off of a lot of suffering in this world and off the world herself as she strains to deal with my 1974 Gremlin's carbon dioxide ...

LIKE MAYBE ... next time we won't be electing the country club trustee Georgie Bush President of the United States and believe me there is waltzing in Washington right now ...

LIKE MAYBE ... it is time for lines to be drawn ... some absolutes to be acknowledged ... some choices to be made ...

BECAUSE ... BECAUSE ... BECAUSE ...

BECAUSE ... silence actually does equal death ...

BECAUSE ... action actually does equal life ... these are not metaphors or gym wear ...

BECAUSE ... there may not be all that much time left ...

BECAUSE ... my strongest art- and life-filled moment last year was a civil disobedience action in front of the federal building in LA. And with each outline of a friend dead from AIDS drawn on the pavement ... pure spectacle was happening ... drums were beating ... hearts were pounding ... hands and bodies covered and gritty with chalk ... trying to make the big picture . . . which more and more seems to be the one that matters most to me . . .

BECAUSE . . . maybe any function of art that does not basically work in some kind of direction toward healing the sick . . . fostering communication . . . easing suffering . . . feeding bodies . . . or saving the planet just ought to get back to an apolitical, conceptual 1980 where it would be much more comfortable . . .

BECAUSE . . . maybe it's time for a lot of art to be quite useful . . .

BECAUSE . . . maybe it's not enough for us to be sad and pissed off for our boyfriends or our friends who are boys who have been lost to us . . . there are lotsa different kinds of people there in that building behind me . . .

BECAUSE . . . last month I walked around the border near Tijuana with my friend Guillermo who told me that on that square mile more people die each year than on any other place in North America. Run over by cars crossing the border. Asphyxiated in the trunks of automobiles or shot by crazed north San Diego County white supremacist lunatics. I know this is just one injustice out of a zillion, but it cannot be foreign to us. This cannot be ignored. It's in our pockets. It's in our beds. It is next door to Sea World amusement park. Shamu the dancing killer whale is watching us to see if we can hook up . . . we homos . . . people of color . . . the undocumented . . . feminist ecologists . . . crazed global performance artists . . .

AND ALL YOU STRAIGHT WHITE GUYS TOO!!! BOTH OF YOU!!!!

BECAUSE . . . there is a place smoldering inside US that wants to learn this lesson WE Americans need to learn about pain and suffering and loss . . .

BECAUSE . . . each of us—writing, agitating, painting, kissing, performing, designing, activating, fellating, detailing, coiffing, public-relating, primping, obsessing, committing, masturbating—

might make a society not quite so stuck on itself and able to speak so fucking glibly about kindness and gentleness!!!!

BECAUSE ... there's no question ... that more lesbian peace activists from Venice will be blown out of the sky over Lockerbie or Burbank ...

BECAUSE ... there's no question ... each of us is going to have to go to someplace like Mexico ...

BECAUSE ... there's no question each of us is going to walk along the beach and find a body or two there in the sand.

(Tim jumps off his soapbox.)

Then it was over. I gathered my stuff. Because you always want to leave your campsite cleaner than you found it. And I went back to the rally. And became part of the group.

(We hear planes crashing and bombs dropping. A rope drops from above—rope ex machina—Tim climbs, huffing and puffing, up to the rafters and perches there.)

We're up here now. We're all up here high up in the sky. We're all having sex with the twentieth century. I am having sex with the twentieth century in a sleeping compartment on an express train in the middle of the night in Texas. It is an affair that does not stop. I try to be faithful to my boyfriend, but when a new crisis or a cute peace activist comes along I have to go out and be with them. Tongue kiss. Wrestle. Caress. Battle. I remember so many things! And some of them even happened! I have licked Mao Tse-tung's balls—sweet-n-sour. I have held hands with the cute southern boy from Atlanta at the Civil War Memorial. I have spanked Oscar Wilde. I kissed that working class fellow by the RAF memorial on the embankment of the Thames. I embraced Mayakovski before his final Russian roulette. I fucked my beautiful Italian boy on the Lower East Side high up on the roof when we were both intensely young. I have been porked by Richard M. Nixon in the

middle of Whittier Boulevard. YECCH! I held my dying World
War I poets machine gunned there on Flanders Field and my
friends and lovers dead from AIDS. Held them like this . . . and
like this . . . and like this . . . and like this. . . .

(Tim does strong gestures of holding and lovemaking.)

It all comes back. The way my father's body felt lying sweaty
in a hammock in the South Pacific in 1944. My mother's breasts
full of milk for my brothers and sister and then for me. The men
and a coupla women that I have laid with and loved—on the
beach, in the bed, in the trenches, or on some long march. It all
happens at once with that fast forward whooosh when I come.
WHHEEEEE!!!!!

It all happens at once and we will all keep having sex with the
twentieth century. It's an affair that my body might not outlive.
It keeps coming . . . faster and faster and faster . . . all at once . . .
and on and on . . . and on and on . . .

*(Tape collage peaks as Tim climbs down the big rope back
to the stage.)*

and on and on . . . and on and on . . . and on and on. . . .
TAPE OUT!!! LIGHTS OUT!!!!

*(The plug is pulled on the sound system. It growls to a halt.
The lights go out in the space. Tim hands out flashlights to
three or four people in the audience to light him for the end
of the piece.)*

I've got one last thing to tell you. It won't take me long.
We're here in the dark. We're back on the train. It is very dark. A
light flickers far away. I sat at a table in the dining car for supper
as the *Sunset Limited* pounded across Texas on its way to New
Orleans. At my table was a heavyset older couple and a middle-
aged black woman. The train had pulled out of El Paso a couple

of hours before and was now rolling into the endless all night of Texas.

I asked the big question, "Where ya headin'?" And so it begins. The couple was from way up in the north part of Wisconsin. The black lady was from Lake Charles, Louisiana. And I'm from right here, LA, born just over those hills. So I have a place too. Just like they do. And now here we are on the *Sunset Limited* heading for New Orleans.

The man from Wisconsin sold life insurance. I asked him what he thought of air travel. He said he didn't think much of it. His wife had raised their umpteen kids in a house they had built in the woods. About twenty-five miles from a tiny town near the Upper Peninsula of Michigan. The black lady was a grade school teacher at a suburban school outside of Lake Charles. She used to live right next door to the school where she taught but then desegregation came along and now she drives ten miles to a fancy white neighborhood. And the stories start coming.

The couple from Wisconsin are retired but they're now volunteer ambulance drivers. There's only a coupla hundred people in their part of the county so they're on call to drive people the forty-two miles to the nearest town that has a hospital. They start telling me and the lady from Lake Charles about their life in the ambulance. And suddenly there in the Amtrak dining car it all spills out. They're telling me the most intimate details of their life in the ambulance—delivering babies, deaths of their neighbors from heart attacks, accidents, a suicide—the usual grunt and groan routine. The woman from the Wisconsin couple tells us how once they got a call for a baby who had stopped breathing. They raced over there and gathered the crazed mother and non-breathing baby and started doing their stuff. The man's wife giving the kiss of life on the kid while he tried to calm the mother down as they drove a million miles an hour over frozen roads. Over and over again he said, "It'll be all right." He said. "It'll be all right."

And the man took over the story at this point. He told us he was driving like a lunatic when suddenly he heard the baby cry weakly, then a good healthy howl, then another, and then the baby kept crying. He told us at the table that when he heard that baby cry, full of life once again, he sat up straight as he drove toward the hospital and held that steering wheel full of happiness. The tears were running down his cheeks cause he and his wife had saved that baby there on the icy highways of Wisconsin.

We were all quiet for a bit after this story. I poked at my bad pot roast and stringy string beans.

Now, the African American lady from Lake Charles hadn't talked too much so far, but she was clearly moved by the couple's story, by the sheer heat of it, and I could see she had something she wanted to tell.

She dabbed at her mouth with a napkin and said, "Oh, I know. I know how these young ones can touch you." Before she had moved to her new school, back when she still taught at the city school in Lake Charles, she had had a boy in her sixth grade class. He wasn't the best student but he was a good boy and she liked him and helped him and he would come by her house do some chores and they would talk.

But then as June came around and it was the last day of school, she knew he would be going off to junior high. That last day he came by to say good-bye to her. They talked like they usually did. When it was time for him to leave, the boy hugged the lady from Lake Charles. He had never hugged her before and he wouldn't let go. She said his little hands were clasped real tight around the back of her neck, like he was holding on for life itself. The lady told us he was shaking so hard as they hugged.

She calmed him down and told him, "It'll be all right. It'll be all right. You can come and visit me whenever you want. Sure you can, honey. You come by anytime." And then she dried his face and sent him home. And off he went.

The next week, while she was hanging up her laundry in the backyard, she heard from a neighbor lady that that little boy had drowned in the lake just a few days after their farewell. And she leaned forward over the Amtrak linoleum and looked at us around the table in the almost empty dining car in the pitch dark of Texas. She told us—she actually said these words staring us each in the eye—"I think of that little scared boy all of the time. I can still feel his cold hands holding on to the back of my neck right here. I still feel them. I feel them right now."

Well, a waiter came and broke the spell at the table. It was time for dessert. And I thought about what I had heard from these people as the train clackety-clacked on and on. And I think of it now too. The man from Wisconsin crying with joy for the life of the baby that is saved. The lady from Lake Charles haunted by the loss of that little kid drowned in the lake.

And as for me, I feel like I'm dancing around somewhere between those two touches. Bouncing back and forth between that life grip on the steering wheel and that cold touch at the back of the neck.

(Tim stands and comes close to the audience, the light of their flashlights washing over him.)

Now, I didn't tell a story of my own in that dining car, but if I had I might have told this. It's a story about a train. Which is as it should be. Around the back of Griffith Park in LA there is a place called Travel Town. This is a park where a lot of old locomotives and engines and Pullmans are kept. It's a graveyard for trains. They're frozen onto bits of track that don't go any-where. I've been going to Travel Town a lot since I was five or six. I've always loved trains. There is something very sad about this place, Travel Town. There's something completely hopeless because these trains can't go anywhere. It's like they're all dressed

up, embalmed and painted and dead, but not buried. It's a sad place.

I was there at Travel Town a few months ago. I was thinking as I walked around that too many people I know are dead lately. Or locked into seemingly impossible battles with a fucked-up world. And I began to feel like maybe I could get one of these trains moving. That somehow with some help from somewhere, I could do it. I picked a steam engine I liked and pulled myself up into the cab. There was a kid up there. He was about six or seven. He looked a lot like me at that age. He was me. There in my Union Pacific train uniform that I wore constantly as a child.

I looked at myself. We nodded to each other but there was work to do. We put our four hands on the throttle and braced ourselves and slowly pulled it back through the rust and layers of paint. I felt the train creak a tiny bit, and then take a breath. The engine moved forward, straining like a fat man trying to get out of bed, rocking out of its cement shoes on those useless rails. I looked back to the train cars attached to the engine and saw lots of people on board. People I know and care about and people from history too. Some of them are alive and some of them aren't, but now we're all on this train.

Up on top of the Pullman, I saw Jesus. He was polishing something.

Down by the track I saw Karl Marx, he was oiling the gears.

And on the passenger car were Gustave and Maria, Fräulein Rodriguez and Vladimir, Doug and the Lady from the Lake.

The wheels are screaming. The steam is hissing. We're moving forward. Faster. Off the track. Crashing through the chain-link fence out onto the Golden State Freeway. Faster and faster. The whistle blows. The conductor waves.

Everybody is on the train.

We're heading for the beach.

Everyone is going to the sea, at last to the ocean.
Everyone is on the train.
Every One is on the train.
All aboard.

(Fade to black.)

My Queer Body

Okay, I can't resist it one second longer—*My Queer Body* is my most seminal piece. And not just because the show starts with me as a queer sperm getting ready to be ejaculated out of my dad's dick—though that's clearly a tip-off. In *My Queer Body* I wanted to weave a funny, scary, and emotional gay boy's alternative creation myth, an odyssey of swimming upstream as a queer spermlet at conception to my first boy-kiss to the ecstatic visions of homosex transforming the state! This show explores the stories that our bodies carry and how systemic homophobia challenges our deepest selves. The performance traces a journey through the most intimate pleasures and pains of being in our bodies in these difficult and juicy times. In *My Queer Body* we have the sweetness of an early love, a date with a boy at the La Brea Tar Pits, and a frightening peek into a volcano and the mortal fears of the time. I wanted the show to reveal some of the secrets that are held in my heart and head and butt and breath. The show ends up with a rousing call to claim ecstasy and imagine a fabulous queer future complete with a black lesbian president. That's it in a nutshell.

In the heat of the times, I wanted to listen to places on my body speak their tales. I began work on this piece by trying to tell the story of my dick. This launched me on a journey to discover the other stories my body has to tell. If you listen carefully, your lips remember their first kiss and their first loss, your body remembers the places of hurt and the places of pleasure. As a teacher of performance this is something I encourage my students to do. I ask them to follow their nose, as it were, to the stories that each part of their body holds. What is the story of the elbow? What happened to make that scar? The story of the teeth? The eyes? The story of your genitals? What part of your body has a story that really *needs* to be told? Is there a place on your body that carries a story so important that if it doesn't get told you might burst? I invite the people I work with to allow themselves to see the most idiosyncratic metaphors of their bodies as fully as possible. For myself, as an artist, I try to do the same thing. In *My Queer Body* I summoned these embodied narratives as a way of figuring out who I am. I wanted to try to reclaim my flesh-and-blood tales from the clutches of those who would try to censor, control, slice and dice them. Even the audience in this show has to get into the act right at the top of the performance by calling out some of the favorite places on their bodies. You know you're going to have a good show if people shout "perineum" or "pussy" without much coaxing!

I created *My Queer Body* during the worst of the AIDS crisis and in the period when my own particular front line of the nineties culture wars, the "NEA 4" controversy, was at its peak. In 1990, I, a wandering queer performance artist, had been awarded a Solo Performer Fellowship by the National Endowment for the Arts, which was promptly overturned under political pressure from George Bush the First because of the lush, wall-to-wall homo themes of my creative work. We so-called NEA 4 (me, Karen Finley, John Fleck, and Holly Hughes), then sued the federal government with the help of the ACLU (if you're not a card-carrying member, become one!) for violation of our First Amendment rights and won a settlement in which the government paid us the amount of the defunded grants and all court costs. The last little driblet of this case was the "decency" clause, which Congress had added to the NEA appropriation under the cattle prod of Jesse Helms. Judge A. Wallace Tashima of the Ninth Circuit Court of Appeals had sagely declared that using the "general standards of decency" clause as a criterion for the funding of the arts was clearly unconstitutional. Right from the bench he had thrown the language out. This could have been our happy ending, except that the Justice Department decided to appeal Judge Tashima's decision to the Supreme Court.

If you read your newspaper in 1998, you know that in their NEA 4 decision, the Supremes decided that it was okey-dokey not to fund "indecent art." The law "neither inherently interferes with First Amendment rights nor violates constitutional vagueness principles," Justice Sandra Day O'Connor wrote in her majority opinion. In a disappointing eight to one decision, the high court hitched up with Helms and his ilk and declared that the National Endowment for the Arts can consider "decency" in deciding who gets public money for the arts. I was grateful that at least Justice David H. Souter showed he was sensible to the reality of how under assault artists have been in this country for the past ten years. He was the lone justice who dissented, saying the law should be struck down as unconstitutional because it was "substantially overbroad and carries with it a significant power to chill artistic production and display." There is no question that that "chilling effect" is as real as the polar ice cap! I hear this from artists and my students all over the country. It's so embarrassing and enraging that the Supreme Court made this decision that undermined the First Amendment.

The ten years of my life during which my performances were scrutinized by right-wing nuts was about as much fun as a colonoscopy! I felt my work be trivialized and misrepresented all over the place. Whole swaths of the country that I used to perform and teach in became off-limits for years. I lost a great deal of work, and the brave arts organizations that did bring me in to their communities often faced ugly scenes at their theaters. Here's an example of how this would play out: I was performing in Chattanooga not long ago. As the audience arrives at the theater, so do the protesters. They set up shop across the street, a motley bunch of a couple dozen men (they have stashed their wives and children at the corner). As the people begin to arrive for the show, they are forced to walk by the protesters across the street, who wave their Confederate flags (the black cops we hired for security don't seem too thrilled about these characters) as they shout at the audience the usual charming greetings: "Faggots! God made Adam and Eve, not Adam and Steve! Sodomites burn in Hell," etc. The children down the street join in these cries. This seems to demonstrate this particular church's version of family values: The Family That Mates Together, Hates Together. There is a mix of the rambunctious spirit of a carnival and the blood-lust adrenaline of a public hanging. The situation is simultaneously absurd and terrifying. This was my version of show business in the nineties: The gala opening nights! The glamour! The bomb threats! The Confederate flags!

I worked on *My Queer Body* as the NEA 4 crisis swirled around me. Court cases, public statements, death threats were part of my daily experience. This wasn't all that was going on in my life. The long battle of the AIDS crisis was at its worst and my ACT UP activities consumed a lot of my energy. It was a time of feeling at total war. A time when I was as likely to be arrested at a demonstration as I was to be rushing to a performance. People were dying by the thousands. The horrors of the Reagan/Bush era were wreaking havoc on queer and artists' communities. The stakes were very high, and it often felt as though the theaters where I did the piece were reaching the boiling point from the hard times we were in.

I remember one performance of *My Queer Body* that I did in the beautiful Yale Repertory Theatre in 1993. There is one point in the show where I wander naked out into the audience, exposed

by the glare of the follow spot as I get close enough to see people. I look them in the eye and acknowledge them as the community occupying that theater for that evening. I see their glasses.
Feel their hair (maybe indulge in a quip about their hair-care prod-
ucts). Notice this audience's wisdom. Discreetly, of course, cruise
a boy. At a certain point, I sit on an audience member's lap and
look into their eyes. My butt naked on their lap. I try to speak
simply to them about this feeling of loss and craziness inside me.

> I AM here with you. My body is right here. I'm sweaty. I'll
> probably get your pants all wet. You are right there. Here, feel
> my heart. I still feel alone. A little afraid of all of you. And I
> could tell you another sweet or scary story like I've tried to
> do tonight. But whatever I did ... it would be a lot wetter
> and messier and more human and complicated than when I
> stand up there naked in the red theatrical light and pretend
> I'm going into the volcano.

I said these words as I sat on the lap of a young man who was
sitting on the aisle (take that as a general warning). I looked into
his face. Into his eyes. This young man began to shake. His face
quaking. His eyes overflowing with tears. He was trembling
intensely but was so present in his gaze and really making contact
with me. I was scared too. I wasn't sure what was going on for
him. How intense was this? What unknown boundary have I
crossed? Have I fucked somebody up?

Anyhow, finally, I got back on stage where I belonged. I
trusted that this had been okay for this young man. After the
show, as is my fashion, I immediately came out on stage to talk
with people. I like to leave the stage lights up and encourage folks
to come up on stage. They can say hello to me or each other.
Before too long there were about a hundred or so people up on
the stage at Yale Rep. They'd hauled themselves up onto the lip
of the high stage or found the stairs and were chatting with each
other, looking around, saying hello to me. I like to have people

feel that the stage is a place where they are welcome. Their bodies belong up there too. I talked to many people as they shared
with me their experiences of the performance or made contact in
some way that was important for them. The young fellow I had
been with in the audience came up and we hugged. I asked him
if the moment when I sat with him had been all right. He said
that it was. It had just been very intense for him because of many
things going on in his life since he had just come out as a queer
man. The performance had opened up some things within. We
hugged again and he went off with his friend.

Then a man came up to me and held my hand. He told me
his lover had died of AIDS in his arms that morning in the hospital. He told me he hadn't known what to do with himself. He
chose to come and see my performance. He told me that the piece
had helped him in a deep way to be with his feelings of loss and
also to claim the life that is in him for *his* future. To keep claiming the life that still breathes in *his* body. We talked for some time.
Holding hands. Tuning in.

Now, clearly, this was a very charged gathering of people that
night in New Haven. I'm not saying this was a typical night. But
during the years I toured *My Queer Body,* every night I stepped
out onto a stage or performance space I assumed that many of the
people who had assembled were in a dynamic and challenging
experience as they took their seats. For many of them, their presence is *literally* a matter of life and death. One audience member
may be dealing with the upheaval of just having come out and
claimed identity, while another may well have buried someone
that morning. I know that both mourning and celebration often
hover quite near the surface of the community that gathers to see
my work. Those charged feelings are quite present in the theaters
when I step out and ask the audience to shout out a favorite place
on their bodies. I know I am a queer performer presenting my
homo-content work in a time of crisis. My work is filtered through
a complex set of political events around the right wing's attempt

to censor lesbian and gay artists. Perhaps this makes such human gatherings more pregnant with this feeling and need. The call to community more pointed. I want to feel the full blast of the humanness of the situation. I want as a performer to be pulled and challenged and to serve in some small way this most human of gatherings. As a theater artist, I look at an audience and assume that each person has just been to a funeral, or just had delicious sex, or was queer-bashed and carries some wounds and some pleasures very close to themselves as they take their seats.

The beauty of these gatherings makes me feel many things as I start to open my mouth and the lights come up. I feel humbled by the audience's openness. Energized by human presence. Shamed by their authenticity. Emboldened by this challenge.

(The houselights dim along with the pre-show music by the Smiths, Meat Is Murder. *Onstage are a bowl of water, a piece of lava, and a surprise wrapped in a red cloth. We pause in the dark for a moment to acknowledge the miracle that these humans have gathered together in this theater. Tim enters, walking through the audience in a follow spot.)*

Hello. Hi everybody. This is my entrance. It's sort of a rear entry tonight. It's the mood I'm in. Actually, I'm here because I need a few things from the audience. Think of this as sort of a psycho-sexual scavenger hunt. As I look at you all here tonight, I can quickly see that you've all been on a lot of those. I need to gather a few things.

(Tim grabs an unsuspecting audience member's fingers. And whatever else strikes his fancy during this section.)

I need your FINGERS! Oh those dancing fingers. They do a rumba! A bolero later perhaps. We summon the fingers to this place. The fingers are here. I need this person's FOOT! Oh foot in black leather boot. Booted foot, do you know there are entire clubs in this city devoted to your worship? We summon the foot.

We need some pulsating BRAINS. There's a bunch of them over here. Have you noticed the brains always want to sit over there on the right? Many open HEARTS here tonight. I see them shining. These open hearts will be much needed tonight. Bring 'em onstage.

Now, this is the first of several audience participation moments in tonight's program. (OH NO!) I know how you love them. This first one is very easy. I need you to call out some favorite places on your body, or on someone else's body, and while you do this I will spontaneously improvise a dynamic postmodern dance. Let's begin.

(Tim actually gets the audience to shout out body parts: Thighs!!! Breasts!!! Lips!!! Other lips!!! This sometimes takes some coaxing. Especially to shout out naughty stuff.)

I think we're leaving a few things out. Don't censor yourselves. Let's work below the belt for a bit.

(Dicks!!! Pussies!!! Butthole!!!)

Good! We have summoned the body! The body is here.

(Tim steps onstage.)

Let's start at the beginning. The very beginning. My dad is fucking my mom. In a bed. Where else would they be? This is suburban Whittier, California. They're young and hot for each other. I'm trying to visualize this. Half of me is inside my father's dick. The other half is inside my mom. My biology gets a little vague here. They're breathing fast. My dad is going to cum any minute. He's thrusting madly. AH AH AH! Suddenly I am thrown out of my father's dick into my mom's body. I am surrounded by thousands of squirming creatures.

I am swimming upstream.

Oh humble dog paddle!

Oh efficient crawl!

Oh stylish backstroke!

I am swimming upstream. As I would swim upstream throughout this life. One queer little spermlet. . . . Fighting the odds. A hideous sperm that looks like Jesse Helms tries to catch me in a net. I elude him! There's a bunch of generals from the Joint Chiefs of Staff who want to kick me out of this fallopian tube. I elude them, as well. Then a bunch of hulking macho slimebag straight-pig sperm shove and try to elbow me out of the way. Call me "Sissy! Pansy! Fag! You'll never find an egg! HA HA HA!"

Clearly this is homophobia. My very first experience. But! I use my superior agility, fleetness, and sense of style and calmly leap from plodding straight sperm forehead to straight sperm forehead. I quickly find a willing dyke ovum, we agree to power share. We reach consensus immediately (this is a fantasy sequence, all right!) and we . . .

FERTILIZE!!!!

There is an explosion of creative electricity. A shifting of queer tectonic plates. Skittering across the well of loneliness to Walt Whitman's two boys together clinging on the sea beach dancing! I see Gertrude Stein is in a tutu. She dances with Vaslav Nijinsky in a butt plug. They do a pas de deux on the wings of a fabulous flying machine created by Leonardo and piloted by James Baldwin and Amelia Earhart. They fly over the island of Lesbos where Sappho is starting to put the moves on the cute woman carpenter who has arrived to build her a breakfast nook.

There is a puff of feathers . . . an angry fist . . . a surface-to-air witticism . . . the off-the-shoulder amazon look! Embodying the bridge between woman and man and back again. The sperm is a fish. The egg is a rocket. Five, four, three, two, one!!!

And . . . ECCE HOMO!!! Behold the fag.

And now the big cry to the universe. It's time to be born. WAAAAHH! The doctor spanks my butt. WAAAHH! He spanks it again. WAAAHH!!! I look back and I say, "Doctor, I won't really be into spanking till I'm at least twenty-four!"

With that first pre-erotic and nonconsensual spank a wave of shame and body fear washes over me. I fight back. I kick the doctor in the balls. Rejecting his authority. I slip on my "Action = Life" Huggies. Slither into my attractive "We're Here We're Queer Get Used To It" powder-blue baby jumper. I see all the other queer babies in the nursery start to shimmer and grow and explode from their diapers. They all grow to adulthood. Some of them find their way to this theater tonight.

Until I stand before you now.

(Tim rubs his heart.)

It hit me right here. First it hit me right here in the heart. Right here. Only later it hit me in the head.

(Tim walks into audience and approaches someone.)

Could you rub me here please?

(Audience member rubs Tim's heart. They get fresh sometimes.)

Well, a lot of things have done that. Hit me in the heart and the head. The election of Ronald Reagan, AIDS, the first time I got butt-fucked. Oh, and the only date I went on with a boy in high school.

(To person rubbing.)

Keep going. A little faster and harder please. If your arm gets tired just switch hands. I'm going to set the stage now. Everyone pay attention. There is a bed there. Right there up on stage. It has a big old pine headboard painted Pin-N-Save antique green. The Vitalis on my father's head has burnt a hole right through

seven layers of paint to the maple wood underneath. My mom's sacred jar of Noxzema is on the bedstand. I always tried to use that Noxzema to beat off with it but you can never get up a good slide with Noxzema. Plus it stings! See, people have tried.

I make a solemn vow never to endorse Noxzema for masturbation no matter how much they try to pay me. This is the bed. The bed I was conceived on. The bed on which I would be born once again. Thank you, nice rubbing-person.

(Tim walks onstage.)

I offer this now in tribute to the first time this meat and bones got close to other flesh and blood. It's the story of the only date I went on with a boy in high school. I met him. Robert. The guy I would go on the date with. I was seventeen years old. He was seventeen. I am thirty-four now, so that means I am now almost old enough to be my own father in this story. It's a stretch, I know, but it's possible. I think maybe I am my own father in this story? Trying to give birth to myself? But I don't want to do that. I really support guys who do. You know, all the cool granola-y straight men with the drums and stuff in the woods. I want to do something else. I want to remember and claim and conjure my queer body at seventeen when my entire body was a hard-on.

Oh, I had a hard-on for Dostoyevsky.

I had a hard-on for Patti Smith.

I had a hard-on for many of the boys in my gym class.

Robert went to a different high school in Anaheim near Disneyland. He grew to his seventeen years in the forbidding shadow of the Matterhorn Bobsled Ride. He was slight and fair, cute, and wore glasses, always a plus. He was the lead singer in a proto-punk rock band based in Tustin, California. They mostly did songs taken from obscure texts of the Marquis de Sade. My friend Lori introduced us. She had met him at one of those bohemian hangs in Fullerton, the left bank of (hyper-conservative) Republican Orange County.

She loved him. But quickly realized he was a big fag and passed him on to her friend Tim. I called him up.

"Hi, Robert! This is Tim. I met you with Lori. Hey, you wanna go to the beach with me and then we'll go into LA to the 'Shakespeare on Film' retrospective at the County Museum of Art? Huh?"

He said he would.

I picked him up in Anaheim with my blue '65 VW Bug. This car was my initiation. My symbol of freedom. I drove the streets of LA feeling the future inside my body and listening to Bryan Ferry and Roxy Music on the transistor radio pressed to my ear.

Robert and I went to Diver's Cove at Laguna Beach. I had been to this beach many times before . . . mostly with my Congregational church youth group. But now everything was different. The sand was epic. Like in *Lawrence of Arabia*. Bigger than a 70mm widescreen movie. Each word we said hung perfect and crystalline in the cool fall air before it was blown by a wind toward Japan. We found a secluded nook and talked. While we spoke, I noticed that he was doodling with his fingers and building a wall of sand between us. While he was doing this, he was saying that he always put up barriers between himself and other people. That he kept emotional distance. The wall was shoulder height now. I said, "Robert, this is so intense. It's such a coincidence. I know exactly what you mean. I feel like I do that too. I put up those emotional walls. But, Robert. Robert, we have to find the way to break through those walls."

And our hands moved through the base of that sand wall and our fingertips touched. Our eyes connected in a Star Trek laser beam of awareness and perfect feeling. Our lips projected beyond our bodies' boundaries. We kissed! The Big Bang.

YES!!!

The triumph over all the times I was chosen last for football. YES!!!

The victory over the tears that ran down my face when my fucked-up cousin would knock me down punching me in the face calling me "Half Man! Half Man! Half Man!"

The times my sister dressed me as a girl—looked like Jackie Kennedy in my wig, pillbox hat and pink dress—and introduced me to our neighbors as her distant cousin Melinda from Kansas.

That confusing ping-pong of feelings when I watched David Cassidy in the *Partridge Family.* I think I love you. But what am I so afraid of?

Our lips parted and we put our tongues in each others' mouths just like you're supposed to. I tasted his mouth. It tasted like . . . hmm. The roof of his mouth tasted like cigarettes. His gums tasted like a child's. His tongue tasted a lot like my own.

We kissed for a long time. He pulled his high school ring off his finger and slipped it on mine. I have this ring with me. I wear it always. The Valencia High Panthers. I treasure this ring as a symbol of perfect love, of course, but also because I really suspect this will be the only high school ring that any seventeen-year-old boy is gonna give me in this lifetime.

We kissed and kissed and kissed again.

The wave crashes on a California beach and the page has turned.

We drove blissfully back through traffic on the Santa Ana freeway past the theme parks. Past Disneyland. Past the Movieland Wax Museum. A cloud hovered over my Bug when we drove by Knott's Berry Farm. Robert began telling me about this affair he had been having with Ricky Nelson. He had fallen from his *Ozzie and Harriet* glory and was reduced to playing gigs at the Knott's Berry Farm amphitheater. They had had a very bad sex scene backstage. This scene seemed to include a large amount of LSD and several enormous summer squash. Should I believe him? I'm not sure. Ricky Nelson queer? Not according to my sources. What is he telling me? That he's scared of sex? Scared of me? I can relate. I'm scared of everything too!!!!

WE WERE YOUNG QUEERS IN LOVE AND WE WERE
SCARED SHITLESS!!!

Some things don't change.

We got back to Whittier and picked up my friend Lori to go
to the movies with us. Now, this might seem strange to you that
we would go on a romantic date with my friend Lori. But, Lori,
though she was not a dyke, was (believe me) the queerest of the
queer kids at my high school. And both then and now the queer
kids (whether they're straight or gay) better fucking stick together.

We were going to see the Zeffirelli film *Romeo and Juliet* at
the LA County Museum of Art. SHAKESPEARE ON FILM! I
had seen it as a little boy when it first came out with my sister and
her best girlfriend who had the unfortunate name of Kay Hickey.
Me and Betsy and Kay Hickey went to the Whitwood cinema to
see it. It was all a little bit much for me with the cleavage and the
heavy breathing so I mostly kept my eyes covered. But, there was
one shot in this movie where I had to look. We see the beautiful
Leonard Whiting as Romeo face down and naked on a bed. His
butt hovering there lunar-like in the soft Verona light. My fingers
intuitively opened over my eyes. I rose from my seat and began
to walk down the aisle. My fingers reached toward the screen cast-
ing ten-foot-tall Panavision shadows onto that perfect butt. I
touched the screen and his Romeo's ass undulated and danced
above me.

And at that precise instant . . . at that moment . . . I enlisted.
I signed up. I am now a career homo officer. Because I knew
someday I would get to see that butt again except the next time
I would be seventeen and holding the hand of my new boyfriend
from Anaheim.

We got to the County Museum of Art and had a romantic
walk (just the three of us) past the La Brea Tar Pits. Now, for those
of you that don't know, the La Brea Tar Pits are primordial pits
of petroleum sludge that are next to the County Museum of Art.
They've been there since the dawn of time . . . or at least since that

field trip in first grade. Anyway, for tens of thousands of years, prehistoric animals, people, tennis balls, and coffee cans have fallen into these pits and been sucked to the center of the earth. Well, it hit me right here. Then right here.

The feeling of eternity that was there in my heart and in my head was so strong. All of those beasts and those people, they were like me. Feeding and fucking. And then they got sucked to a tarry death. This put us in the proper mood for the movie.

We walked down Wilshire and into the movie theater. We sat in the front row. The lights dimmed slowly . . . slowly. The movie began.

(Yes, dear reader, we now hear the haunting, melancholy music from Romeo and Juliet.*)*

I sank down in my seat. I slowly reached over and grabbed Robert's hand. I had never watched a movie while holding someone's hand before. It's nice! I see why people like it so much. You might wanna try it right now. That feeling of connection. A lifeline back into the world as the movie rolls and rolls.

And what a movie to watch on your first date with a boyfriend. It had everything. Poetic language. Fabulous sword play. Doomed love. MICHAEL YORK!!!! Now, what is going on when a coupla fag teenage boys hold hands and watch *Romeo and Juliet* at the LA County Museum of Art? There is a survival technique about how we manage to see who we are. Sure, we enjoy all the cute Italian boys stuffed in their tights and bulging cod pieces. But we also project ourselves into the film. Take in the images. Become them. Use them. I was always really good at this. Sometimes I was Romeo/Tim hanging with his friends. And then I would be Juliet/Tim throwing herself on Romeo/Robert's chest. And then I would be Mercutio/Tim, so obviously in love with Romeo/Robert, if you do a careful textual reading. Then, this was my favorite one, once again I was Romeo/Tim and I was gonna run away with Mercutio/Robert. I was gonna heal him of his pain, so haunted by Queen Mab. We'd go someplace safe and good . . . like the Renaissance Faire in the San Fernando Valley or something! We'd build a life together there at that Pleasure Faire. We'd get a little duplex over a tallow-maker's souvenir shop. There'd be a big fluffy bed with feather comforters. We would take our clothes off and rub our bodies together. Loving the touch of skin. Just like I would when I was a little boy. I would come home from church and take off all my clothes, the suit the tie and the tight shoes, and put my naked little boy's body between the polyester sheets. Loving the feelings on my skin. Making them mine. Reclaiming my body from church and state.

I remember. I remember.

But, then, the sword is pulled. The shit happens. Everyone is torn from everyone they love. And there is a plague on *all* our houses.

The movie ends and all are punished. The lights come up slowly.

It's very quiet as we leave the movie theater. We walk silently out past the tar pits. I wander off by myself through the trees down to the chain-link fence surrounding the pits. I look at the moonlight sheen of water hovering over this eternal life-filled goo. I stare across the tar pit lake toward the giant plastic sculpture of the woolly mammoth in his death throes.

It's been there as long as I can remember. Then, I see something. The woolly mammoth opens his eyes. His trunk snakes out into the night. He lifts one massive leg. Tar dripping from each woolly mammoth toenail. A rapier pierces through the tar. We see Tybalt and Mercutio and Romeo and Juliet rise out of the heavy sticky stuff, hover a bit, and whisper to me . . .

Live these days.
Love well
Value every kiss.
And savor your body's blink between being born and dying.

They wave at me and sink slowly back into the unforgiving tar pit. Only the woolly mammoth is left. I see him wink at me and then he throws his trunk and tusks back in a permanent plastic death trumpet. I shake my head and the vision is gone.

My friends call to me. I run to join them. I want to explain to them what I have seen. I dance in front of them, leading them down the path past the bone museum. I leapfrog over the bronze saber-toothed tiger. Climb up on the back of a mastodon . . . and crow to the night.

And yet I wish but for the thing I have:
My bounty is as boundless as the sea,
My love as deep; the more I give to thee,
The more I have, for both are infinite.

(I knew these lines by heart because we had the soundtrack LP to the movie.)

We fall on each other and run galumphing toward my VW. I open the passenger door and Robert gets in the back and Lori in the front. We laugh and scream and joke about stuff. We are just so glad to be together in a car in Los Angeles in 1976 and not in Verona in 1303. I drive a little bit too fast down Sixth Street toward La Brea. I keep trying to catch Robert's eye there in the back seat. I wanna kiss him right then. I want to keep the connection going. Stay the link.

(Shocking blast of a follow spot. Tim is pinned to the wall.)

THEN IT HAPPENS.

It's a wild panic-filled slow-mo. The crunch of metal. The breaking of glass. I'm thrown forward. It hits me in the heart as the steering wheel takes my breath. And then it hits me in the head. My face becomes stars as I hit the windshield. Just in time to see Lori break the glass with her forehead as Robert is thrown between the front seats cutting his face on the rear-view mirror. The horn is stuck blowing. The woolly mammoth in the tar pit

hears it and tries to come save us but he just sinks deeper toward death. Gas is leaking. Tires are spinning.

Why, God? Why, on my only date with a boy in high school did I have to rear-end a hopped-up maroon El Camino at forty-five miles an hour, thus totaling my beloved Bug, ruining my date and my entire life? WHY?

Questions careen. Can I get the car home somehow? Is anybody hurt bad? How will I explain this? Do I look like I have been kissing a boy all night long??? We get out of the car. We're all basically okay. But my beloved Bug is dead. The woolly mammoth can't help me now. Who will save us? I'll call my father.

I walk about two inches tall to a phone booth on Fairfax and call my dad. He arrives shortly after followed by a tow truck. I don't think my dad does a big shame-on-you routine, but I definitely could be repressing that. The tow truck takes my Bug away and we pile in my dad's Datsun to drive home in complete silence.

My mind races. I plot to myself how to salvage this evening. I look at Robert. All I want to do is lay down with him and kiss him. I start to improvise plans and strategies. Finally I have it. I say, "Dad, it's very late isn't it? You know, I was thinking, Anaheim is twenty minutes past Whittier. It would really make more sense for Robert to stay at our house tonight and then you and I can drive him home in the morning."

Pretty creative, really, under the circumstances.

My dad raises his eyebrow. Seventeen-year-old boys do not do sleepovers. All he said was, "AAAARGHHHHHH!!!!!!!"

English translation subtitle of Angry Father Language, "OK," appears over the stage. We get to Whittier and drop off Lori. We get to my house. As my dad tries to open the front door with his keys, my mom keeps locking it on the other side. I decide to use this Freudian moment for the second part of my plan. I say, "Gee, Dad, we're both pretty upset from what has happened. Traumatized, really. I think it would be best if Robert and I sleep in the same room tonight."

My dad raised both eyebrows, but all he said was "AAAARGHHH!!!!!" Translation: "whatever." Which was as close as we were going to get to a blessing that night. Now, I know I said "same room," but what I should have said was "same bed" because there was definitely only one bed in my room. Yes, that's right. This was THE bed. The bed I had been conceived on. My parents had recently gotten a new giant double king and I, ever the drama queen, thought I would like to sleep on "The Bed I Was Conceived On."

Robert and I shut the door to my room and I locked it with a chair under the doorknob. We stood there real nervous. Then it happened. The miracle of life. We opened our bodies, walked toward each other, hugged and kissed. This is it. This is it! The best thing we get while we're in our bodies on the planet Earth. I felt it in my heart, where the steering wheel had taken my breath. I felt it in my head, where my face had smashed the glass. And now I felt my love and desire for this boy rise up from those two places on my body.

We took off our clothes but kept our underwear on and got into the cold bed. I think that at that moment, as my skin hit those sheets and I naturally moved to hold my friend's body, that at that moment maybe I became a man. This might have been the moment. Maybe I am a man now with a man's ways.

I comfort my boyfriend as we lay down at the end of a hard day.

I will soothe Mercutio who in this story does not die from his wide and deep wound.

I will honor the little boy I once was who had the good sense to wiggle his body naked between the sheets after church.

I will hold that boy and that man close to me throughout this life.

We kissed for a long time. Our hands owning each other's bodies. But, then, Robert pulled away and looked at me and said. "You know, Tim, I'm still pretty fucked up from that bad sex scene with Ricky Nelson at Knott's Berry Farm. Is it okay if we just hold each other and kiss and don't do a big sex thing?"

Well, I didn't care. This was enough of a miracle for one night. The woolly mammoth had taught me that. I am happy to smooth that other rough touch with my gentle kiss. That out of the crash. The explosion of metal on metal. The face breaking the glass. That the end of day has brought me to this bed with a scared and (except for his JCPenney white underwear) naked punk rock boy filled me with such feeling.

He looked me in the eye and we kissed. And kissed. And kissed again.

His senior ring on my finger.

His hand on my heart.

His body next to mine.

We slept together on THE BED.

And I was conceived once again.

(Tim rubs his heart as lights fade to deep green. Breathes loudly and moves with the text.)

My skin is a map.

A map of my world. My secret world.

It tells you where I've been. And how to get to where I come from.

It charts my seas . . .

my peninsulas . . .

my caves . . .

and my mountains.

I travel with this map over my skin.

I go on journeys. Find new coastlines. Hidden borders.

I follow my nose along the touch that has pulled me through life.

I lead with my tongue.

I go by foot . . . by dick . . . by brain sometimes.

I know the path by heart.

The pleasures I sailed across.

The pain I pointed toward.

The knowing my bends and hollows.

The bodies . . . many bodies . . . I have touched and been taught by.

The secret places soothed and stroked.

But, then . . .

"X" marks the spot.

(Tim stomps.)

There is a plague and hatred on the land.

An earthquake within.

Whole continents have been lost to us . . .

The Island, that no man is . . .

A hemisphere carved out of my fucking heart . . .

Then the burning began.

Burned up those carefully drawn and protected maps.

This fire spread over our skin.

Boiled our seas.

Burned up my city of angels.

The flames spread to the tar pits. Smoke to the sky.

And burned. And burned. And burned.

(Follow spot catches Tim as he is thrown again and again against the wall.)

And a COP threw me against that same chain-link fence— where the woolly mammoth had winked at me.

And a COP threw me against that same chain-link fence— where I had pressed my seventeen-year-old cheek trying to see love for another boy.

And a COP threw me against that same chain-link fence— when thousands of us queers marched to the County Museum of Art after our slimebag Governor Wilson had vetoed the state lesbian and gay rights bill last year. We marched there pissed off and strong because we felt like it. Shut down our city. Trapped the governor inside that museum while he giggled nervously sipping champagne in front of a Rembrandt.

(Tim walks down an aisle into the audience.)

A lot of things happened in those days. Some good. Some scary. When we started tonight we called up some places on our bodies. Some things happened to those places too. Somebody said fingers . . .

(Tim touches people with each body place, marking the audience.)

Your fingers were smashed by a horse's hoof when hundreds of LAPD cops on horseback trampled through us hurting a lot of people. Your beautiful arm struck with a cop's nightstick.

Your wrists swelled real bad from the tightness of the handcuffs after you were arrested and were kept in the basement of the parking structure at the Century Plaza Hotel. Your beautiful ass got dragged along the pavement. All our spirits battered by the fuckheads in charge. My face up against the wall of art.

I watched this happen here at my tar pit as they surrounded us, hundreds of LA cops on horses. Hurt. Hit my friends. Bully with horses. Everything rushed in.

So many friends and lovers dead from AIDS. City of plague. Government of hate. Vain and crazy men in power. The war they make on our bodies. My body's in a state. The state of California? I saw the flag of my state burn many times that night. The last time it burned . . . at the last possible moment the California bear that is on that flag jumped off walked over to me and said, "Tim, let's get outta here."

Now I firmly believe that if a bear jumps off of your burning state flag, you should do whatever it tells you to. I took a drink.

(Tim drinks from bowl and picks up big piece of lava.)

Gathered my personal effects and followed the bear down Wilshire Boulevard. Everyone was frozen where they stood, the activists and the cops, just like in a bad mid-seventies science fiction film starring Charlton Heston. I followed the bear for a long time down Wilshire Blvd. For about two years. I grew tired and couldn't stand. I crawled on my knees. I eventually collapsed in the parking lot of a Denny's restaurant in Barstow. I lay there with my face on the broken glass. But then a graceful Denny's waitress with big hair came to me. She cradled my head on her mustard blouse and spooned weak spoonfuls of coffee with non-dairy creamer into my parched lips. And then she sent me into the desert.

I crawled through sand along a wash. The sand went into my skin. Into my bones. Into my blood. Into my breath. Until I became just a speck of sand. And was blown by a hot wind far east into the Mojave Desert until I came to the Amboy Volcano.

AM BOY.

It's a real place. I'm not making it up. A scar on the horizon. A wound open to the sky.

Is this the mouth or asshole of California? Great chunks of lava. Black and grimacing.

Looking like angry clenched faces.

This is the volcano of my family. I came here with my dad when I was a little boy. The only time we went on a journey by ourselves. Left the City of Angels. Had breakfast in Barstow. Passed through the wreckage of Baghdad on old Route 66. Walked the lava fields of Amboy. Went through Needles. Crossed the river to King Man. King Man, Arizona ... where my grandfather homesteaded a ranch.

This is the volcano of my family. A frayed snapshot in 1919 of my grandparents passing the volcano on their way from the farm in Kansas to a new life in California. My dad and I wandering in the lava fields of Am Boy. My brother knowing I would come to this volcano once again.

(Tim dangles the big lava rock over his head.)

This is the volcano of my life. It has a sharp point and it hangs over my head. I walk toward this volcano with my dead father. I walk toward this volcano with my dead boyfriend John who came to this desert to try to heal himself of AIDS. I walk toward this volcano now with my living boyfriend these ten years, Doug. Even though I'm alone.

This is the volcano of my life.

I crawl up the side of the volcano. Every step I take I sink up to my hips in ash and blasted bits of bone. I feel like each step might be the wrong one. Might shake the earth to its soul. Break its heart. The lip of the crater is high. My breath races. There are cocked Eisenhower-era hydrogen bombs and exploded Frigidaires everywhere. Bits of bone blasted from the center of the earth. The smell of rotten grease blasted from a place for burning.

I get to the top of the volcano.

I didn't go into the volcano when I was here with my dad when I was little. But I will now. I did what you're supposed to do. I stripped myself naked.

(Tim takes off all of his clothes and stands in red light.)

Bared my heart to the hot sun. Hoping that it might warm the frozen places. Dug my feet into the earth. Ash between each toe. Under each toenail. It felt like an old friend. So familiar. Like the ash we will all become. Bared my dick and butt to the sky. Took a walk around that crater and far in the distance I could see a billboard for the Bun Boy Restaurant in Baker, California. "We are the Bun Boy Restaurant. We have the best biscuits in all the Mojave."

What is inside my volcano?

My fear . . . stronger than life. Sometimes. Who taught me that?

My shame . . . deep as the sea. Sometimes. Who gave me that?

I'm knocked down. I am grabbed and pushed and shoved along the top of the crater. A hundred hands tear at me.

Blood pours from here and here where my first major lover David was stabbed nine times with an icepick in front of a gay bar in Garden Grove. QUEER! QUEER!

Blood pours from here and here where my boyfriend Doug was bashed almost killed with the two-by-four and the blood pours over our breakfast linoleum. FAG! FAG!

Blood pours from here and here where the catheters pierced my friends' sides so the medicine could go in their bodies. AIDS! AIDS!

Broken here where Reagan and Bush smiled their do-nothing holocaust grins while my friends died.

Broken here and here where my own embarrassment twisted my spine and threw me off-center with the feeling I'm no fucking good.

Broken here and here why is it . . . when I am about to kiss a boy I have been flirting with on Santa Monica Boulevard do I have to imagine an unkind god above me is going to throw a rock at me and smash my head.

Broken here and here dick and balls smashed off by the hammers of Helms and Buchanan and Sheldon and Wildmon.

Broken here and here.

Butthole blown open by DIRTY DIRTY DIRTY they said. DEATH DEATH DEATH they said.

Blow winds. You're cracking my fucking cheeks.

I'm dragged down into the crater. Pinned there at the bottom. Naked in the crater. My butt and hole up to the sky. Dick buried in ash. My mouth is full. I whispered secrets into the earth.

I miss my friends and lovers who have died.

I am afraid of my mom's body.

The tumor on my side kept my shirt on for fourteen years.

He was so thin. I was so scared.

Don't watch me take a shit.

What are my father's secrets?

I miss the dicks that were up my ass that are now ash.

I am embarrassed that I am alive sometimes.

I lay there for nine years. Watching my friends and lovers die before my eyes. Then, a horrible beast came into the crater and crawled toward me. It opened my body. Tore at my skin. This beast started pulling corpses out from inside me. Hundreds of them. I recognized every face. It pulled these friends dead from AIDS out of my butthole. Piled them like wood in this giant crater. Filling the hole. The wound. All around me. I was being buried. They were gonna block out the sky. Up here. Up here.

I'm gonna stop there. If it's okay with you I'm gonna stop there. Actually, even if it's not I'm gonna stop there.

(Tim calls up to the tech booth.)

Hey, up in the booth! Could I have that bright follow spot light we had before?

I made all that up. All that about the volcano and the beast. I lied to you. I'm sorry. Don't hate me. I don't really know what's in my volcano. I don't know much of anything anymore. The only thing I really know is that I'm here naked in front of all of you right now.

(Tim walks naked down into the audience.)

That becomes even more tangible when I walk in the aisle. I'm here with you and you and you. I *see* you. Even without my glasses. Which are very strong.

(Tim touches someone's hair.)

This person has nice hair. A little too much mousse, maybe. I could learn something from you. You look wise tonight. Many cute boys here. Can I sit down here?

(Tim sits naked on someone's lap.)

This is the most nervous part of the performance. Here, feel my heart. I see my face reflected in your eyes. I am here with you. I AM here with you. My body is right here. I'm sweaty. I'll probably get your pants all wet. You are right there. Here, feel my heart. I still feel alone. A little afraid of all of you. And I could tell you another sweet or scary story like I've tried to do tonight. But whatever I did . . . it would be a lot wetter and messier and more human and complicated than when I stand up there naked in the red theatrical light and pretend I'm going into the volcano.

See, I can shove through the bare-assed shame. I'm pretty good at that. But I still feel more of my friends slip away so what good is it? After ten years of being scared and angry. No wonder I gotta go into the volcano sometimes. Some nights I feel this strange border between my body and some friends who are really sick right now. It's a coastline I don't like. I want to throw a surf-rider to them and pull them to shore . . . but I can't do that. Who am I kidding? I wanna tongue-kiss them, and I do, even though I'm afraid. I wanna hold our bodies really close together so nobody else slips away and that I can try to do . . . that I can at least try to do. And I'm really glad cause I don't think I can manage much fucking else.

Please nobody go anywhere. I have one more thing I gotta tell you. It won't take long. I swear.

(Tim goes back onto the stage.)

You want a volcano. I'll give you one. Up here on stage there are the outlines of hundreds and thousands of people who have died of AIDS. Some of them I know. Some of them you know. You walked across 'em on your way to your seats. Do ya feel them on your shoes? It's a strange crater we're in and there's strange fruit here.

This one is Martin and I've told his story before but it hurt much more in real life and the sex was better than I let on.

This man was Keith, drawer of pictures on the subway, and we sniffed around each other and made love a few times in a tiny bed in a room with no windows when we were both intensely young and wanting to be famous artists on the Lower East Side.

This was John. A man I loved but not well enough and left and whose face I see in my mirror and on the faces of my friends if the light is right. And whose body I still feel inside of mine just like it was that one blizzardy Sunday in New York before the snow got real dirty.

Now these three are just my boyfriends. The men whose dreams I shared, art we made, lips I kissed and dicks I sucked.

There are dozens of other friends here. People I know or you know. Now, I shout myself hoarse. I've ACTED UP all over. I wash my hands. I put up my stickers. And I'm still here and I'm fucking glad of that but it means the world makes no fucking sense. I am not USDA choice anything. Why am I breathing *right now, tonight*, and they are not?

Now that's a big fucking question. And I'll get an answer if I have to go into twenty volcanoes or pull God down here by his too-wide lapels and slap him around until I get some answers.

Because I don't understand this pain and this loss anymore than I did ten years ago.

Because I try . . . but sometimes I am still the same selfish prick who ran for the hills when love walked into the room.

Because I've lost my maps and I don't know where I wanna go on my body.

Because we're all gonna die. Right? We all know that. We all bought that ticket. We all signed that lease. We all got our volcano, but, meanwhile, I am here in my body. I gotta find the chant, the rhythm, the offering, the ritual to be here in my body and remember what is gone.

In my breath up here. My spirit all around. To not close my heart. My legs right here . . . through my feet to the center of the earth. My cock in the world. My belly my friend. My arms up here. My brain on fire. Up here. Up here.

(Tim stands still. Pause. Tim looks at his forlorn penis.)

Uh oh. I've got myself in trouble again. I'm naked in front of all you people. Painted into a corner without any clothes on. Plus my dick looks so sad and forlorn. So abandoned. So soft and so shy.

Pssst. Hey you. You missed your cue. You know you were supposed to get hard after the psychosexual empowerment litany.

Look I'm really sorry. This *never* happens to me. It'll just be a second.

(Back talking to his penis.)

Are you trying to make me look bad? Don't talk to me about performance anxiety. GET HARD! Ooops. We all know, in this situation, yelling does not help. I'm going to work with you. Directorially. Okay. I'll suggest some stimulating and arousing imagery and then you'll get hard and we can leave the volcano. You can all do this now in your seats or later in the comfort of your homes. We are in a field. A plain. Warm and sensual water moves across this field. Reeds and grasses dance in the wind. Beautiful and muscularly defined golden retrievers running through that high grass. Sal Mineo and James Dean are there naked having hot sex finally rewriting the last scene from *Rebel without a Cause*. NOW GET HARD, GOD DAMMIT!!!

What? You say not until I finish my story? Okay. This is a fairy tale. Maybe I can make up a new ending and maybe we'll find our way out of the volcano. Now, in that volcano, the corpses were pulled out of my butthole for a long time. Some corpses were found that everyone had been looking for. Jimmy Hoffa. JFK's assassins. All eighty-six of them. An important object, too. The Holy Grail. But I had always known it was there.

Then it stopped. I was spent. I bent over and smoked a cigarette. Then I felt something moving through me. I squatted down over the earth and I gave birth to an EGG! Well not an egg. It's a seedpod, obviously. Wait. I know this seedpod. I know it well.

I left Philadelphia, the City of Brotherly Love. I walked over the river to New Jersey. I walked for many miles. I came to a cemetery. I found the grave I was looking for. At this crypt there were poems, flowers, offerings of food. This is Walt Whitman's grave in Camden, New Jersey. The moment I stood in front of this grave this seedpod fell from a tree far above and hit me on my head. Inside it were many things. Inside it was a high school ring. The breath of every man I've ever kissed. And a light that could change the end of that old story that tells us our bodies are good only for death. Well, that's my story. It had a magic seedpod ending. That should be enough. So now you'll get hard and we can leave this place and I'll tell you why.

Get hard because it still feels good to be touched . . .

get hard because there is so much that is gone . . .

get hard because even though it's not the most important thing it's magic when it happens . . .

get hard because it's the least we can do . . .

get hard because you can remember you are alive . . .

get hard because every time I come I think of the men I've loved who are dead . . .

get hard because once we're gone we can't . . . I think.

Get hard because we can't let the right-wing fuckheads tell us how to fuck . . .

get hard because I want these boners before I am just a bag of bones . . .

get hard because there's work to be done . . .

get hard because I am a queer and it is good and I am good and I don't just mean in bed . . .

get hard because it is time to make a move. To transubstantiate. A little alchemy please. Let's turn that rock into gold. The water into wine. The pain into change. The bus is arriving. The alarm is going off. Because I only know one thing. This *is* my body! And these are all our times.

So . . .

Get hard . . .

Get hard . . .

Get hard . . .

I hard-ly know what to say . . . except that we're here in the greenish glow again. I'm gonna use this greenish moment to pull up my pants. You'll have to use your imagination for the rest. You might wanna arrange yourselves in case you got a little damp or bulgy. Well, come on, it could happen, it did in Cleveland! Whatever you do, I need you to do it quick. I need your help to help me create a little alternative reality. We have to project a bit into the future. Not too far into the future . . . otherwise it's just too depressing.

Okay. Back at the volcano. I said, "Fuck this Jungian mythopoetic stuff. My queer friends are getting beat up back at the museum." I rushed back to the tar pits. Everybody unfroze. As you know, that night we forced the governor out of office. He works in the copy room at the Lesbian and Gay Center in LA now. This created a firestorm of change throughout the nineties during which queers, people of color, and women made enormous advances until finally at some point early in the new century the United States elected the first black lesbian president.

This is where I need your help. We are no longer in this glamorous theater. We are now at the Kennedy Center in Washington D.C. It is the inaugural gala for the first black lesbian president of the U.S. She has appointed me performance art laureate of the nation. As you might imagine, I have accepted. But she has given me a very serious challenge. She has commissioned me to create a symphonic homoerotic performance art cantata that will exorcise homophobia and bigotry from our land. Basically she wants me to create a work that will, via a global satellite TV hookup, explain to the planet how fabulous it is when two men have sex together. The lesbian a capella group from Portland, Maine, will be doing the same thing for dyke/dyke sex in the second half of the show. I have been working with the LA Philharmonic for weeks in California and then here in the District for the last ten days. There is tremendous excitement here tonight; both houses of Congress, the Supreme Court. I'm going to put on my evening clothes now. The lights in the Kennedy Center dim. They dim. Oh how they dim. There is a buzz of anticipation in the hall. From ten thousand lips this buzz comes. Make a buzz please. I step out onto the stage; there is immediate thunderous applause.

My conductor, Zubin Mehta, steps to the platform. We exchange a meaningful, yet private, personal gesture. And I begin.

Good evening, as performance art laureate of the nation, I bid you welcome to the inauguration of the first black lesbian president of the U.S. I offer this piece in memory of all our friends who have died of AIDS and in honor of the breath and pleasure that exists in every body here tonight.

Music, Maestro Zubin.

(The music comes up. Yes, it's Ravel's Bolero. *Please, dear reader, imagine the music brewing toward climax during the rest of the performance.)*

You look at him . . . sometimes over your shoulder . . . sometimes across the crowded performance art space . . . you make the signals . . . a glance held too long . . . a leg in contact not pulled away . . . the sharing of knowledge . . . the crucial questions . . .

"Didn't I meet you once at ACT UP?"

"Weren't you in that performance piece at Highways?"

"Do you have a boyfriend . . . if so do you sleep around?"

These are the politics of our space and how we bridge it. Close. But not close enough yet. Not for this reporter. I want to *know* this man. What he tastes like. The books he reads. The touch he has. A little neck massage is not out of order here . . .

OR PERHAPS
A QUICK GAME
OF POSTMODERN
MID-PLAGUE
TWISTER.

But, finally, the lips touch. I kiss this man. Oh good. Who will stick his tongue in first? Him or me? Who cares! A little two-day beard on the faces as they rub and EUREKA we know we're guys. All right, I admit it. It's that sandpaper cha cha that gets my fingers snapping and does a soft-shoe on my slutty heart. The hands grab each other close in a real embrace. So close that no junior high chaperon can shine light between us. You feel each other's backs. His hair. His butt. With pelvoid radar beginning to feel the hard thing. . . . Oh that lovely hard thing, in the pants.

A coupla bumps in the night start to rub over each other before the embrace pulls away. You look each other in the eye. It's scary isn't it? Don't pull away.

I SEE YOU NOW
HELLO I'M HERE
Hands move over chests.
Get the lay of the land.
The cut of the cloth.
Pinch the nipples.
Which, yes, we do find get more sensitive with each passing year. . . .
One of the many benefits of getting older. . . .
What is inside my heart?
What have we here inside this second-hand Walt Whitman breast?
There is so much LOVE!
We roll the foreheads together.
Pinching each other's tits.
A breath or a "yeah" showing what feels good.
Beginning the spar.
And let me hear a "yeah."
Good! This is *not* a joke.
Not to be kept at arm's length with a nervous laugh.
This is ground zero. A crossroads. The vortex.
THIS IS
THE HIT PARADE
My hands reach down and feel the particular hard dick there in the pants. This is a big moment.
Sort of like the lottery.

And I don't give a shit whether they're big or small. Black or white. Cut or not.

Through thick and through thin, I am just glad to be lucky enough to be feeling this particular hard cock at this troubled moment in history, if you know what I mean.

Our hands go under shirts.

The tongue-tips ... touch ... down ... down ... the neck. . . .

The fingers open the shirt, a bite on the nape, a nip on the nipple.

The other hand negotiates the buttons or zipper. Struggle with the belt or Velcro tabs. I hate this part.

And finally reach in.

Oh it's hot and sweaty here.

Where the underwear mashes the curly queer hair.

Then you reach down and grab low under the balls.

Feeling them heavy like a scoop of ice cream.

AND PULL THE DICK

UP AND OUT

The pants may now get cheerfully dropped,

depending on your fashion.

Shirts get pulled over the head and then ...

Oh skin, skin, skin—thank God for skin.

Our pants are open and our hearts uncovered as we get ready to bare our souls and buttholes.

Cocks mushed against bellies.

The tongue-tip trails down to the tit,

up to the pit.

Redrawing those maps with our tongues on skin.

Down to the place where the pubes and the dick hook up.

Where the freeways meet. Where the turf meets the surf.

Then the tongue goes up Interstate 35 up up up and around the shaft. Tongue-tip dances along that cock. The mouth is open. We pause there now for station identification.

RIGHT THERE
AT THE TOP
Safe sex quandary moment. Is it or isn't it?
Only your urologist knows for sure.
To suck or not to suck. That is the question.
Let's be serious. . . . Let's be honest.
Let's assume, of course, we're gonna take a little journey up
and over that dick for a while at least.
This is a special moment.
A sacrament of sorts. Made more sacred for our fears.
Speaking of fears, I don't taste any pre-cum.
(I once had to explain to a straight woman friend what pre-
cum is. I told her . . .
"It is the rustle of wings
The rumble afar. It is the taste of things to come.")
And when that dick is in my mouth or my dick in someone's
there is a faith in the universe and the rhyme comes out right.
AND IT GOES DOWN
LIKE HOME COOKING
And hands go up and down and around the town to a visit
to the balls so pleasant and bouncy.
And we're up and there is a kiss.
The fingers now do the walking and the dance down under
beyond the balls to what my friend in Texas calls . . .
(He was a cute boy who I had sex with in a hayloft in San
Antonio. I lured him back there with my classic pick-up line,
"Hey, wanna ditch the party and go out back and look at the
chickens?" Well, that's another story.)
Anyway, he told me that where he comes from this area is
known as the "'tain't," the area between dick and butthole.
The scientific word being perineum.
It is called this, and not just in Mississippi and East Texas,
because "'tain't your dick and 'tain't your butthole."
It doesn't matter to me what words you use.

WHATEVER YOU CALL IT
IT IS GOOD
And then the question . . .
"How much does each of us want our buttholes to be played with and what will we find when we get there?"
I know this is a nervous subject so let's assume we have both been swimming in a highly chlorinated pool for seven hours doing the breast stroke. So when we get down there things are extremely tidy and puckered and cool.
Our fingers go around and converse, flirt with our buttholes. Getting to know you. Getting to know all about you.
And a "yeah" is called for.
Which is an affirmation of our place in the universe.
Everybody take a breath . . .
LET ME HEAR YA SAY *YEAH*
PUT IT IN!
And the democracy of fingers.
We all got 'em. Lots of them. Enough to go around.
Ten times ourselves.
And we got 'em inside each other now. No one on top.
The bottom pulled out from under us like a sly slapstick rug.
The other hand is on each other's dicks.
The finger goes in and the held hand goes up and lips are pressed.
And we fall down and over and about.
And head to foot.
Lip to ball.
Finger in butt.
We're in a universe of our own making.
No more waiting.
Our hoped-for escape from gravity. Weightless.
We're in our own solar system.
PLANETS IN
OUR SEXY ORBIT
Don't you see?

This is the promised land where your lips . . . all of them
and your points . . . all of them
and your holes . . . all of them
get tended and loved.
Get their valves adjusted and their licenses renewed.
It's like this sex will revive the big identity document that says "I am! My body belongs to me!"
Flipping the bird to fear.
Because even though there has been so much death, we are still here with our skin and bones.
There is blood and spirit and queer horndogginess within and about me.
Between you and me. Between your butts and your seats.
Between our hearts and our heads.
I AM IN MY BODY
I AM IN MY LIFE
I've got a hard-on for the universe.
Sometimes a yielding unclenched butthole that might keep the world from blowing itself up. . . .
And don't tell me this white boy don't have rhythm because that's all it is now.
It's all listening and sensing . . . and reaching . . . and reaching.
And someone reaches for a condom.
They're never where you put them.
There they are. Oh reminder of plague we embrace you!
Someone opens it with slippery hands
(this has a 9.3 level of difficulty)
and slips it over, pinch at the tip . . . roll it down.
Down. Down. Down.
THE AIR IS OUT
AND THERE IT IS
And, now, let's flip a coin or consult the oracle.
Check the tea leaves in the tea room and one way or another a dick is going to find its way into a man tonight.
And this is no small thing.

It makes the world turn upside down.

This pleasure that one man can and will give another.

A dick in a butthole.

A whole lot of peace.

A piece of ass.

Now, what is the problem here?

Is this the love that dare not show up on network TV?

Is this the sex that launched a thousand ships and burnt the topless towers of Washington?

Is this the butt-fuck that put bees in the bonnets and tent poles under the cassocks of cardinals in Columbus?

Are we stuck with their images? Their projections?

Their religion?

IS IT ALL OF *THEIR* THINGS???

No. For once, right now.

It is just ourselves.

Two men inside of each other without a knife, a gun, or a stock portfolio.

And one is close. And then another is closer yet.

Full. Fuller. Fullest.

There is a nod and a yes and a squeeze and breath.

I am fucking I am being fucked. Every single cell.

And heads or tails I am glad to be here my body in the world.

The water inside me.

The dying that comes to all.

And it is faster and closer than we knew.

Everything that we hoped for on the jungle gym . . .

hanging upside down and twirling around and around

on the highbar of our lives.

Naked between the sheets after church.

THE CURTAIN RISES

AND THERE WE ARE

Naked in the sight of each other. The only ones that matter.

I am fucking I am being fucked. Touched and touching.

Time now to know each other and ourselves.

I am fucking I am being fucked. And so close.

The words in my brain fly out the windows like a bunch of crazy birds let out of their cage.

I am fucking I am being fucked. Right there.

There is wetness and hardness and growing together and quick in my heart and my head.

I am with you now. And with my friends and lovers who are dead from AIDS. And with all the queers who got burned up in the concentration camps. With all the dykes and homos bashed on the streets of our fucked-up country. And for the little fag within me who cried so much as a kid and never does now. Not anymore.

(The Bolero *builds, becoming really loud.)*

But, now, I feel the blessing of being closer than they told us was possible. The fuckers lied to us. I am not ashamed of nakedness and I will not be cast out of Paradise by Jesse Helms or some fucking hunky archangel with a flaming sword in front of some garden.

(Music totally blaring.)

This is one sex between two queer men's bodies
in the time of trial
on the planet Earth
at the very end of the second millennium.

(The music ends with almost a flash-bulb moment of climax. Then blackout.)

Naked Breath

I wrote *Naked Breath* because I wanted to do a performance that was full of the raw, intimate stickiness of blood and cum. I began working on the piece shortly after getting beaten up by the Houston police during my visit there with ACT UP during the Republican National Convention in 1992. We dragged ourselves back to the Motel 6 just in time to see Pat Buchanan making his famed "culture war" speech on the TV in the smoke-filled bar. This lovely encounter with the Spirit of Texas was the cherry on top of two years of being battered around as a First Amendment poster boy, as one of the NEA 4.

A bit the worse for wear, I created *Naked Breath* at a time when I definitely needed to let some light in. I had begun to doubt some of my own slogans and the in-your-face street activism that had fueled me for a number of years. My response to how AIDS was hitting my life began to be really intimate and full of memory, sex, and sorrow. This mood set the scene for this work.

Also during this time, my partner Doug Sadownick and I were primary caregivers for singer and AIDS activist Michael

Callen. Michael and I had planned to collaborate on this performance and had been awarded a Rockefeller grant to bring it to life. Sadly, Michael died before we had a chance to complete the songs for *Naked Breath*. I felt haunted by the loss of Mike as well as so many other friends and lovers.

I was drawn to two different events in my life that happened on East Sixth Street in Manhattan. One was in 1981, the day that I had bled the most, when I cut off the end of my finger while working as a carpenter. It was a day that ended with me walking back from the hospital down East Sixth Street with my boyfriend of that time, John Bernd, the dancer and choreographer. At that final moment before the AIDS era began, it was a day full of portent, humor, and twenty-eight stitches in my right arm and hand.

Somehow I knew I needed to throw this story in the blender with another day that had me walking down that same street in 1992. Eleven years later, and frayed from the culture war and onslaught of AIDS, I was again walking down East Sixth Street with a man I had just met named Andrew, on our way to a romantic collision. On that totemic East Village street, I soon found myself in a sexy and highly intimate space as two men—one HIV-negative, the other positive—managed to connect in a time of plague. After several years of shouting in front of government buildings or being dragged by cops down the asphalt on the streets of Los Angeles or Houston or San Francisco or New York, I felt called to really honor the quiet human-sized victories that are available to us. I wanted to try to locate what has happened to us during the AIDS era and hold up the hopeful fact that men were still able to get close to one another there amid the swirl of blood within and the cum smeared on our bodies. In *Naked Breath* I am surrounded by both of these bodily fluids; I wanted to get wet in this performance.

Speaking of wet, one cool, fall evening a few months before the premiere of *Naked Breath* I was walking along the sea where I live in Venice Beach. It was the day after Thanksgiving and I watched the sun slowly set, slipping into the unruly, gray Pacific.

The days were getting short, shorter, shortest. I walked along the foamy shore. A wildly cute surfer dude peeled out of his fluorescent wet suit to a moment of nakedness (I was having a religious experience at that point) and then he wiggled into his baggies. An older African American man on roller blades dressed like Santa Claus whizzed down the bike path playing "First Noël" on his electric guitar in the fading November dusk.

A certain sadness hits me hard as the light diminishes in the weeks before the winter solstice. I believe somehow as the days get dark that we are called to become aware of light, to witness it in a deep way. To open the curtains and raise the blinds. Of course we do this again and again in performance. Fade to black, and then we have the miracle of a bright light coming up downstage left. The early nineties were dark and rocky times for our queer tribe. The relentless roll call inside our heads kept asking, "Who's dead? Who's depressed? Who's left?" These questions were wearing my incisors down to the gum line. I needed to nudge my political rhetoric and find a way to say "thanks," to life if nothing else. I needed to see the narrow places where the light was still shining, bright enough to warm our hearts and heads.

That fall of 1993 Doug and I had spent Thanksgiving with Mike Callen and his family in his room at the hospital. We had eaten turkey and played cards, as good diasporic midwesterners do. Later, I sat with Mike on his bed watching him and Doug talk as I listened on headphones to a recent sound-studio mix of Mike's song "Love Worth Fighting For," which we thought we might use somewhere in *Naked Breath*. Mike's delicious voice wrapped around me and held me close as the music soared. I saw Mike and Doug talking. Their mouths moved silently; my ears filled with Mike's song. I was graced by such a feeling of luminescence, love. Even there, as my friend Mike was being knocked around by the final troubles of his twelve years with AIDS, his voice shone through on the tape as he and Doug held hands on the bed at Midway Hospital in Los Angeles. The light was shining.

Mike Callen died a month after that hospital Thanksgiving and he never saw *Naked Breath*. My goal as I created the piece was to be sure I didn't miss any of that available light. I didn't want AIDS or the fucking radical right to make me miss a single bright ray that I was lucky enough to witness. The light from seeing my queer friends be good to each other. The light from hearing our voices raised in song or protest or performance. The light from the look-each-other-in-the-eye heat of our queer sex, which truly *is* worth fighting for. And the light from our ability to sit on hospital beds and be together even in the hardest of times.

I continue to hear Mike's voice so often in my life. Of course I hear his four-vowel bel canto riff on the word "loathsome." I can't forget that. But mostly I hear his songs like a comforting wind, a breath that I want around me. I keep hearing Mike's voice as a guide to how to be a queer man, lover, and faggot artist. *Naked Breath* is dedicated to the memory of the fierce spirit of Michael Callen.

(The stage is bare except for a giant sunflower in a heavy glass vase. Tim enters from the back of the house breathing in and out very loudly. He checks to make sure the audience is breathing too. He stomps on stage and the lights come up.)

I'm breathing. Are you? How about you? Everybody take a breath. Let me hear. That was good.

Now take a nice breath through your anuses. Here. I need to do a spot check.

(Tim approaches some audience member who is probably dreading just such an event.)

Would you breathe on my wrist? Would you breathe on my heart?

(Tim locates a special someone for the next bit.)

On my dick? OOPS! I'm getting ahead of myself. Time for a tattoo, I think.

(Tim pulls a Magic Marker out of his pocket and sits on the lap of an audience member and asks them to draw on him.)

Could you tattoo my arm please? Just write NAKED BREATH in bold Virgo clear letters and then put a heart around it and an arrow through the middle. Here's a Magic Marker. Ya know, they say that with every breath we take we breathe in a couple of molecules that Leonardo da Vinci once breathed. I have always believed this. I choose to believe this because it makes life more interesting. But that also means that with each breath we make we also breathe in some molecules from Atilla the Hun . . . Mary Tyler Moore . . . Pop-N-Fresh?

A coupla molecules from Jesus on the cross. A coupla molecules from the guy I had sex with last week and he breathed so deep. His skin so beautiful. A coupla molecules from Bill and Hillary and what I hope is still their loving bed. A coupla molecules from each of us gathered here.

Thanks for the tattoo. Wow.

(Tim leaves the tattoo audience helper and is back on stage.)

I'm gonna breathe you in.

I'm gonna breathe in your warmth and the miracle of human presence in this room. You all got here! No one got hit by a car on their way to the theater! I don't take it for granted, believe me.

I'm gonna breathe in the colors and ages and sexes and haircuts and fashion choices in this room.

I'm gonna breathe in the multiple piercings and even the presence of the butt plug this gentleman in the third row chose

to insert before coming to the theater tonight. (Not much gets past me, doll!)

I'm gonna breathe in the wish that some of you have that tonight you'll meet someone go home together have sex and become life-connected.

I'm gonna breathe in the sadness. Oh it's here too. Sometimes hiding there in the seams of our trousers and the hems of our dresses.

I'm gonna breathe in the joy. It's different for each. The joy of the morning cup of coffee! The joy of the blow job! The joy of the favorite song! The joy of the touch that matters.

I'm gonna breathe in the heat that is reflected from that time last summer when you lay in the sun as naked as a shorthaired cat.

I'm gonna definitely breathe in the voice of Mike Callen. He was a singer, activist, and the ultimate diva I've ever met. His songs are with us here tonight. I'll float with his breath.

I'm gonna breathe in the memory we carry of the others that have died. Some of our lovers. Some of our mothers. Some of our brothers.

I'm gonna breathe in the blood and the wood and the sacred beds in Grammercy Park that are in this story tonight.

I'm gonna breathe in the grace of each beat of our pulse. Each snap of our fingers. Each rise of our chests. Each breath we make.

I'm gonna breathe you in and I'm gonna let your breath carry me down a street. You know we all have a street inside us. (It's the first metaphor of the show. I'll give you a moment.) It's a place where some things happened. I'm gonna let you carry me down that street now to a time that was a time for building.

As my hand reaches down behind the upstage left black curtain (you're not noticing this) and grabs my very special . . .

(Tim craftily grabs a hidden electrical circular saw and gets it going. Loud!)

Of all the approved boy activities of childhood, the only one I was really good at, other than beating off fourteen times a day, was carpentry. It was the one place my dad and I connected, where his expectations and my homo predilections could look each other in the eye and exchange a manly handshake.

Under my dad's watchful eye, I built bookshelves, napkin holders, birdhouses that no bird thought were safe to go into, and glamour-filled split-level tree houses decorated with throw rugs! I'd invite my little friends into my treetop lair, pull up the rope ladder, and try to convince them that we should cover ourselves in corn oil and play naked Twister.

I loved going to the lumberyard with my dad. It was like church. Better. More authentically spiritual! Sackett and Peters Hardware and Lumber in Whittier, California, was a gothic cathedral of two-by-fours, a delicate abbey piled high with a maze of construction-grade plywood. The sunlight slipping in between the spindly fir strips dappled our bodies as my dad and I searched for just the right piece of maple wood. Most important, lumberyards were staffed by sexy men in sleeveless orange fluorescent vests showing their great arms. Their job was to meet your every woody need. The lumber workers sauntered godlike as they led you into dark hallways to offer you their mahogany. They'd turn the plank over in their hands, show you the wood's true line, stroke the smooth sides, measure out in inches exactly how much you needed.

Then they would take the wood to an enormous table saw, a fierce machine that could rip and tear the wood. In an explosion of grating sound, the sawdust covered your body. The sensation tickling my skin and the earthy smell of a shower of sawdust made me shiver with pleasure. I breathed it deep inside me.

In my life journey through teenage blow jobs, Synth/Pop music, the Reagan/Bush years, and the rise (and fall) of the Queer Nation goatee, I have always tried to stay close to my carpenter roots. When I was nineteen, I moved to New York City and began the usual scoreboard of crummy jobs.

First I was a bellboy on Central Park South. Every Tuesday the retired dentist on the fourteenth floor (it was really the thirteenth; could that fool anyone?) would push his bourbon-drenched face into mine and try to kiss me. "You can't kiss me in the elevator, Mr. Rothbart! Think of your wife! Your grandchildren!"

I spent two weeks as a falafel maker on MacDougal Street. The owner, a Hungarian with a heavy accent, criticized everything I did: "You stupid boy, you must put humus evenly on *inside* of pita bread. You would have been worthless when Russian tanks rolled into Budapest!"

I worked with my new friend Mark, who shared my interest in performance art, as a juiceboy at a busy midtown healthy eatery called the Curds and Whey Cafe. The unctuous manager explained my precise time schedule to me: "From 9:05 to 9:08 you collate juice filters. From 9:08 to 9:11 you take the carrot inventory."

Now, my parents did not raise me in the Golden West to become alienated labor back east. Finally, I gathered my tools, chisels, saws, hammers, sexy carpenter belt, and I started my own carpentry business. I became a builder of beds. With a newfound entrepreneurial zeal, I designed an advertisement which I Xeroxed that had the look of a kidnap note: CARPENTER-PERFORMER-HOMOSEXUAL AVAILABLE TO BUILD LOFT BEDS THAT WILL CREATE A NEW YOU! The phone started to ring almost at once. I built hundreds of beds for the people of New York City. Now, in New York, no one really has space in their apartments to sleep properly, so most folks with tiny apartments more sensibly decided to have special raised sleeping shelves in their apartments that were called "loft beds" whether they were in a loft or not. Somebody had made up the word in an effort to make it sound glamorous, like we were in Paris: "Darling, let's retire to the loft bed, have a cappuccino, and bump our heads." Clearly there would be a market for my loft bed construction business.

No solution to the space problem was too bizarre for me: I'd build my loft beds anywhere. I'd build beds in hallways. In closets. A bed built out over the stove in a studio apartment's kitchen was very practical in a Lower East Side tenement without heat. You could make some potato latkes and keep yourself warm in bed at the same time. One loft bed I craftily hung from the ceiling by chains attached to meat hooks in a bedroom painted slate gray. This bold design became very popular on certain streets in the West Village and Chelsea. The reassuring stability of the chains provided numerous secure places for bondage toys which solved that age-old problem that has confronted mankind, "Where do I attach my handcuffs or wrist restraints so I don't have to pretend I can't escape?"

I would build hundreds of beds for the people of New York City. Beds for people to sleep on. Beds for people to fuck on. Beds for people to get pregnant on. Beds for people to get sexually transmitted diseases on. I had found my vocation. I was a husband of sex! A maker of sleep!! I took Manhattan to bed!!!

Okay, running your own carpentry business when you're a young fag performance artist takes much too much work. Trust me on this. The burden was too great, Manhattan too vast, the money too meager. So, in the summer of 1980, I gathered my saws and hammers and chisels and sexy carpenter belts (I had two now—one for day wear, the other for evening), and I found a contractor named Frank di Martini who needed an extra hand. He hired me and my life as a Brooklyn construction worker began. I now became a part of the subculture of a small construction company in Brooklyn. It was such an intense testosterone scene on the construction jobs, a mix of carpenter-jocks, ex-hippies, intensely butch dyke union wannabes, and one fag. All of us shared one thing: we were all good with wood.

Frank di Martini was a compact, pony-tailed, rippling-muscled sensitive New Age guy. He insisted on having at least one sweet and emotionally tuned-in gay man on every construction crew. I suppose that was me. This was Frank's version of a sort of queer affirmative action. I think he mostly wanted to have someone to talk to at lunch about things of mutual interest: metaphysics, love trouble, the latest Sondheim opening on Broadway. Frank would share with me the feelings that crosscut his life. Drilled into hidden places. Chiseled into his sense of self.

There was a darker side to this, though. I think Frank also wanted to have access to my Homo Sensitivity Gold Card. We are all given those plastic cards at birth, whether we know it or not. Frank thought he could borrow it from me if things got bad. It might help him meet his emotional payroll. We would use it to divide our feelings into lines on our lunch break over foot-long submarine sandwiches.

Okay, I know there are some people who would criticize me for idealizing this male universe I had landed in. They would say to me, "I think you are giving too much energy to a basically oppressive heterosexist job situation!" They might have a point, and I may be destined to end up on Oprah Winfrey's "Queer Carpenters Who Give Too Much on the Job" episode.

Sure, I was giving, but I was also getting. I was getting the vibe of a world of working men in Brooklyn. Part of me had always wanted to be accepted by these guys who reminded me of my brothers and cousins. It was sexy too, being surrounded by all these straight men and their tools all day long. Mostly, I was out on the construction sites, except, of course, when hardened union guys from Queens were around. I was honored that in some way my queer gifts were being acknowledged and honored there amid the whir of the saw and the bam-bam-bam of the nail gun.

That first day on the job with Frank we did eight hours of demolition in an ancient basement on Adelphi Street. Yuk! The Pleistocene dirt of Brooklyn covered me from head to toe. This grime was made up of the grit of the writing of Walt Whitman and Hart Crane. At the end of the day, covered in their poems and black soot, I sat on the D train heading over the Brooklyn Bridge back to my home on the Lower East Side. I caught a glimpse of my face in the shutting subway door. I didn't recognize myself. I was filthy from the day's work. There was a raccoony splotch of white where my face mask and goggles had been. I looked like those Welsh coal miners in the classic 1941 film *How Green Was My Valley.*

At the first stop in Manhattan, some artist friends got on the train and sat across from me. As they chatted amiably, they had no idea who I was. They didn't recognize me. I had become the invisible worker, someone who earns his keep with the sweat of his brow.

(*Over the sound system we hear, naturally, the Red Army Chorus singing "The Internationale."*)

Before too long, in that crucial summer of 1980, I became the head co-foreperson carpenter at the People's Convention in the South Bronx, a protest shanty town designed to expose the hypocrisy of the middle-of-the-road Democratic Party, who were having their convention in New York City that summer. My partner foreperson carpenter was a fabulous dyke named Marty. She is a performance artist today too! Marty and I were Dyke and Fag Carpenter People's Heroes, ready to build a new social experiment there in the bombed-out South Bronx. Later on in that summer, Marty and I would march with thousands of others in defiance of the corrupt Democratic Party Convention at Madison Square Garden. I took off my red plaid sleeveless shirt, the one I always wore on the construction sites, and waved it over my head to show my politics and attract the cute man with the trust fund representing the Socialist Worker's Party. We poured past the Garden as we manifested our demands for social justice! Economic empowerment for all workers! We will seize the means of production!

(*The Red Army Chorus fades down to a whimper.*)

I do miss communism every now and then.

But my friends on the subway couldn't see any of this. They probably thought I was just some working grunt on my way back to the wife and kids in Washington Heights. Had they only looked closer, though, they would have noticed the Manifesto Red nail polish I was wearing that particular day. I had crossed over from my art life, and I now dwelt in a different world. I was now part of this realm of dirt and dust and beer and . . . blood!

Earlier that afternoon, while the jackhammers had pounded, Mike from deepest Brooklyn was starting to space out after his five-foot-long submarine sandwich lunch and four Budweiser and two Amstel Light (because he was dieting) beverage break. His blood sugar was not doing well at all. At about 2 P.M., he slipped on a rock and his Sawzall, which was on at the time, tore a hunk of meat from his leg. Screaming in pain, he was hustled off to the emergency room. Those of us remaining exchanged nervous glances as Frank picked up a bucketful of sawdust and threw it over the spreading red pool of blood and said, "Back to work."

Now, every carpenter knows this is the tightrope we walk. These tools that can cut through brick and wood can also cut through our meat and bones. It is a blood contract, and nobody really knows the terms of it.

While I was going to Brooklyn to rebuild brownstones throughout 1980, I was also seeing a man, this guy named John. I met John because I saw a postcard up in the Laundromat on Second Avenue for a performance art piece he was doing. It caught my eye during my spin cycle. John was so beautiful with his mess of androgynous curls glowing in the photo. His dancer's arm was held extended out to the side, fingers reaching all the way to New Jersey. I had to meet him. I got his phone number.

"Yes, in Manhattan," I said to the telephone operator. "I'd like the number for the attractive man on this postcard doing minimalist dance." (Directory assistance is amazing!)

I called John up. "You don't know me," I said, "but I think we should get together and talk about the new directions for gay men's performance in the eighties. I'm putting a festival together at PS 122." Okay, so it's been a recurrent pick-up line in my life.

"It sounds interesting," John said cautiously. "Why don't you come over and we can talk about it."

On my way to John's apartment in the East Village, I walked down East Sixth between First and Second. This is the block with all the Indian restaurants. Shagorika. Kismoth. Taste of India. Passage to India. The Gastronome Ghandi. Ghandi to Go. They're all there! I used to imagine that all these restaurants shared the same kitchen. I was sure there were block-long conveyor belts delivering huge piles of poori and papadam like stacks of laundry to each small restaurant. In those soon-to-arrive delusional paranoid days with the election of Ronald Reagan, I was convinced that one of his operatives (Ollie North, perhaps) was going to sneak back there with his clutch purse full of plutonium and dump it into the common vat of mulligatawny soup. In one fell swoop he would wipe out all the queer performers in the East Village because these cheap restaurants were where we ate.

I got to John's house, 306 East Sixth Street. He buzzed me in.

"How many flights is it?" I shouted as I climbed the many stairs leading to John's apartment.

"Just keep on coming," John called down. "You've almost made it."

"Whew," I gasped, "That's quite a hike."

John extended his hand.

We had tea. We ate cashew chicken from the one Chinese takeout restaurant on the block. I was very drawn to John, so I cast my net wide and tried to pull him to my shore. John resisted me. I think he knew I was going to be big emotional trouble, so he struggled to avoid the coastline of my side, to miss the shoals of my chest, not to get pulled down by the undertow to my dick and butt.

John tried, but it didn't work. Sorry.

Who's the fish and who's the lure really in all of this? I don't know. I know we sat on wood boxes. John and I shifted near each other, and the inevitable thing happened, the only thing that could have happened between John and me: We began to fall toward each other, obeying the law of gravity and the even greater law that governs falling bodies. It was like when NASA's Skylab was going to fall from outer space and crash to earth. They could try with all their might to keep it from falling, but down it came anyway. Nobody really knew who the debris would hit when it plunged into Western Australia. What if a big piece had hit a future boyfriend of mine, then a little boy in Perth dressed in a Catholic boys' school uniform? I didn't care where Skylab fell as long as it didn't hit me or anyone I love *personally* in the head.

That kiss with John happened as we hit the earth's atmosphere. Then came the opening of clothes and the rush of feeling as we entered each other's undiscovered countries.

"Can we go into your bedroom?" I asked, a little uncomfortable on the wood boxes.

"You want to?" John asked, rubbing my close-cropped hair.

"I think so."

There was a voice inside of me that was telling me to wait. I wasn't sure if I had a passport for this journey. *My papers probably aren't in order. I'd better turn back. I'll just leave now. Well, on second thought, maybe John and I can just sneak over the frontier at night. Hope for the best.* So we kissed. And ate each other's buttholes, of course. And fucked each other.

That night as I slept next to John, I dreamed so vividly the dream came with specially composed dream-sequence music. I dreamed I was in a graceful world, rolling fields of grass extending as far as the eye can see. Feeling John in bed next to me, it seemed that this was a world we might get to live in together. On these fields of grass was humanly designed architecture, like the perfect college campus, the University of Iowa, maybe. It was all the colleges I never got to go to. I walked through this grassy dream looking for John while strange and beautiful music played from hidden speakers in my head.

John didn't want to love me. But I forced him to. For a while it gave him a lot of pleasure. Later it would give him a lot of pain. But for now, for a few powerful months together, how we loved to fuck each other!

I should get back to work. The first weeks I was seeing John, Frank di Martini and Company was doing a job in the Fort Greene section of Brooklyn. We had undertaken a massive renovation, and now I was working all alone on this site, doing the finish work on some doors and the parquet floor. Most people don't know that I am an expert door hanger. (I know, it's a fascinating subject.) Now, door hanging is a very useful skill because everybody needs doors. We need doors to go from one room to the other, sure. But we also need doors to go from one time of life to another. So if you know how to make a doorway, you'll always have work.

I had framed out a door at this brownstone and had left a space above for a transom. I was waiting for the stained-glass artisan, who was late (as artisans will be). Finally Gene, Mr. Stained-Glass, arrived with his wide grin and wider shoulders. His long hair and two-day stubble made him look like one of the cuter of Jesus' disciples just fresh from a workout lifting rocks in the desert. He stripped to the waist as he installed his piece . . . of glass. I pretended great interest in how he was deftly placing his work of art. It gave me a reason to be close enough to him to sniff the aroma coming up from his shucked-down overalls. The stained-glass commission he had fulfilled was a sort of reedy-lake-mallardy-duck-on-the-wing thing. We admired it. Then, out of the corner of my eye, I saw he was admiring me quite obviously. Then Gene the Stained-Glass Hunk spoke.

"So . . . uh . . . do you like being a carpenter?"

"It's okay," I replied, flinging a slug an electrician had left on the floor.

"You really seem to have a knack for it," he said, examining my rather skillful work on the doorjamb.

"I'm good with wood," I replied, looking him in the eye.

Well, with that line, he had to make eye contact, right? So he glanced up and moved slowly toward me, brushing a fleck of wood off my cheek. His hand reached around my shoulder, and he pressed his body onto mine as we leaned against the door frame. The heat of his body made my face turn red like a bursting cartoon thermometer.

"You really know how to hang a door," Gene said. "Let's see if it swings."

Suddenly, we were kissing and grabbing and poking. Soon, our cocks were in each other's mouths as we stirred up the sawdust below our feet. The smell of the wood was in my nose and on my skin. It took my breath away. We offered each other our mahogany. We turned each other over in our hands. We showed each other our true line. We stroked our smooth sides. We measured out in inches exactly how much we needed.

It was clear to me that Stained-Glass Man was about to come on my pricey birch-veneer clamshell molding. I breathlessly said, "Not there! Shoot on the inexpensive knotty-pine door saddle!"

We both came by the door hinge. Lazy dollops of cum, like a dentist's office abstract expressionist painting, meandered slowly down the length of the wood. We looked at each other and laughed, brushed each other off, and pulled up our pants. Stained-Glass Man chuckled, hoisted his tool bag, pecked me on the lips, and went off to his next delivery.

I grabbed some sawdust and threw it on the dripping splooge. I got down on the floor and rubbed the queer cum into the arrogant pride of these rich people's brownstone. Put that on your croissant, Class Enemy!

For the last part of my job that day, I needed to shave one thirty-second of an inch from the back of some of the pieces of parquet floor to fit flush around the door. For this job I was going to use my hand electric planer. A hand electric planer has eight to twelve razor-sharp blades whirring five million times a second. It's basically a death machine. Now, this was not exactly a case of using the right tool for the job. In fact, it was completely the wrong tool. But since I'd enjoyed an unplanned sex break, I was in a hurry and needed to finish up.

I carefully held the first piece of parquet floor between my fingers. Errrrrh! One thirty-second of an inch off. Good. Glued and installed. I gripped the second piece and carefully brought it close to the whirring blade held in my lap. Careful. Careful. Careful . . .

Now, if we were looking at this scene from outer space, what would we see? We would see a young queer carpenter in a hurry about to make a grave error. From space we would see the swirl of sawdust from where their bodies had recently been, the lingering heat of these two men's mingled breath as visible as any nebula's gases on the opening credits of *Star Trek: The Next Generation*. From outer space we would see that in 1897, the Italian workman in the Bronx who had fashioned the piece of parquet floor had noticed a hard little oak knot there on the underside. Uh-oh. I want you to all watch that oak knot very carefully now as it moves toward that leering blade. Closer. Closer. Closer . . .

The knot hit those blades, the machine jammed, and my hand was pulled into the planer's teeth. Blood spurts everywhere: a tidal wave of gore. *I have cut off my entire arm,* I think. *No, my arm is still there. My hand. No, my hand is still there. My fingers. No my fingers are still there. Wait, the end is gone. I've cut off the end of my finger.*

What could I do?

On automatic pilot I decided to go St. Something-or-Other, the Catholic hospital by the De Kalb entrance to the subway. Now, I believe whenever you cut off a part of your body, you should first find it, then put it in a teacup of ice, and then remember to bring it with you to the hospital. They can do amazing things with these cut-off parts. (I've seen the John Wayne Bobbitt penis restoration video.) I picked up the bloody tool and poked through the blades. I found the cut-off piece of finger, but it seemed like it wasn't going to be much of a help. It didn't look so good: sort of like a little spoonful of steak tartare. I left it in the electric planer.

I tore off my red work shirt and wrapped it around my squirting finger. Bursting out the door, I ran down the street leaving a trail of blood behind me. If anyone was looking for me, they'd know where to find me that way. Each drop of blood there on the pavement was for someone in my life. This one, for John. This one, for Frank di Martini. This one, for me. All these, for everyone here tonight.

As I ran down the street, I remembered all the jobs I'd done in this neighborhood. I put two doors in that brownstone for a Wall Street stock analyst. I made the cabinets in a bathroom in there for this fuck buddy of mine. I was proud of the window sashes for the yuppie family across the street.

I finally arrived at the Catholic hospital and rushed breathlessly toward the emergency room, my hand clutched to me like a relic of the one true cross. I burst through the doors and screamed, "I've cut off my finger! I'm bleeding to death!"

Everyone in the emergency room was screaming too. The nurse and orderlies were weeping and throwing themselves on each other. This seemed an extreme response to my, admittedly, bad problem. But they weren't paying any attention to me. They crossed themselves and said "El Papa" this "El Papa" that.

Finally, a formidable nurse with a faint mustache and the name Ramirez on her breast screamed over the loudspeaker, "The Pope has been shot in Rome! Let us all pray." They all fell to their knees.

My mind took this in and quickly made a checklist of the situation: *I have cut off the end of my finger. I have run bleeding through the streets of Brooklyn. I have come to a Catholic hospital emergency room six minutes after Pope John Paul has been shot at the Vatican! Is this fair, God, really? We have to talk.*

An old woman with cataracts was weeping uncontrollably next to me as she grabbed at me, thrusting her rosary into my bleeding hand. I had never felt more like a WASP in my entire life. Finally, the commanding Nurse Ramirez glided toward me. She gathered me unto her and put me in an examining room. Capably, she placed my whole hand, red shirt and all, into a metal bowl and poured a bottle of antiseptic on it. She began to peel the cloth away, unwrapping my finger like the Mummy revealing himself. My finger was chewed up pretty seriously. It looked like I had stuck it into a garbage disposal and then dipped it in a bowl of salsa ranchera.

Nurse Ramirez remained calm. "Young man," she told me, "we're going to cut off some skin from your arm and sew it onto the end of your finger."

My eyes replied, "Yes! You're beautiful, Nurse Ramirez."

She grabbed a scalpel and neatly cut a nickel-sized piece of skin from my upper arm. Peeling it off like a Band-Aid, she then flopped it onto the end of my finger and sewed it on with deft strokes. The flesh winked shut as Nurse Ramirez stitched the wound closed.

"Sit!" she ordered me. "Keep your finger extended over your head. Wait here for twenty minutes, then call someone to bring you home."

The woman with the rosaries sat next to me. She was calmer now. Patting my shoulder, she said, "I will pray for you even as I pray for the Pope." The TV news reported to all assembled that the Pope would live and so would I.

I waited exactly nineteen minutes and then walked slowly to the pay phone on the wall. I called John and hoped he was home.

"Hello," John said sweetly after the fifth ring.

"I'm in a Brooklyn emergency room," I panted. "I cut off the end of the finger. I'm lucky I didn't die. Please help me." I felt the tears start to come.

"I'll be right there, okay?" John knew to say the right thing. "I'll get there as soon as I can and I'll bring you home."

I don't think any words had ever soothed me so much in my life up to that point: John will bring me *home* to the East Village.

"Okay." I stifled a sob, wanting to be a big boy. "Hurry."

A half hour later John walked into the emergency room. I can still see him now, this most confusing man in my life. I can see him like he is in front of me. John's beautiful face, so generous with his smile. His brown curls tumbled down his forehead and made a place that I would have liked to hide in. John had on his old winter coat even though it was May. It was cinched up with a wide belt.

"I guess my finger slipped," I said, holding up my enormous bandaged hand. "Do you think we can use this in a performance?"

"Don't think about that right now," John cooed. "Let's get you home."

John helped me up from the plastic seat, which was damp from my nervous sweat. We went outside to Flatbush Avenue, the afternoon light making Brooklyn look good, and John hailed a cab. This was a luxury not usually indulged. Feeling special, I nestled down into the seat like it was a stretch limo and leaned my face against the window as we crossed the Manhattan Bridge. The suspension cables framed my view of New York, chopping New York's skyline into little shapes, like the slices of pizza John and I loved at Stromboli's. These bits of Manhattan visible through the thick bridge cables were manageable bite-sized pieces, just like the end of my finger back in the electric planer.

The cab left us at St. Mark's and Second by the Gem Spa newsstand where I often browsed in the porn magazines. John quickly bought a half dozen bialys for us to snack on from the woman at the Second Avenue bakery who loved us and pretended we were yeshiva boys.

Walking quietly down the street, I felt so old. I leaned on John. I felt scarred and scared by this day in my life. I looked up at the buildings of the Lower East Side. I had built beds in so many of these buildings. And I'd had sex in all the rest. I knew their insides. I knew where the studs hid under plaster walls, waiting for the nail. I knew which brick would take which exact spike. I knew what dwelt there in the mystery under the floorboards, the dark places between the joists that we walked on every day of our lives.

I had sawed and screwed. I had nailed and pounded. I had opened my body, and the blood had started to pour. I would try, but I would never be a carpenter again. I might even build another bed or two, but I would never *really* be a carpenter again. But I would always know, inside me, that there had been a brief time in my life when I *was* good with wood.

We walked on to East Sixth Street. I felt the sticky blood still on my arm. On my pants. On my shoes. I felt this blood on Sixth Street. It was slippery under my feet. It was hanging over my head. I saw my boyfriend John that day in May of 1981 on East Sixth Street. I looked to the East River. For an instant I saw the blood that was about to rise up from that river. I saw a wall of angry blood that would sweep away so many, that will sweep away John. I saw this for a second, a deluge about to come.

John nudged me and asked, "Are you okay?"

"Oh, yeah, I'm fine," I replied. "Can I stay at your house tonight?"

"Sure."

We walked into his building and climbed up the stairs very slowly. We went into his apartment. John carefully took the clothes off of me and helped me into the bathtub in his kitchen. He took his clothes off too and then got in behind me. The water surrounding us both, John washed the blood from my body.

(The lights fade to a deep blue. Tim carefully slips his clothes off until he is naked in this light. We hear Michael Callen singing the song "They Are Falling All Around Us." A performer who has been seated in the front row slowly rises from the audience and walks toward Tim. He carries a bucket with water and a wash cloth. He sets the bucket down and he slowly washes Tim's body as Michael Callen sings. He holds Tim close when he is finished and

then quietly returns to his seat. As the song ends, Tim speaks.)

We're walking down East Sixth Street. In December of '92. Eleven years later and eleven years into the plague. How many times in my life had I walked down East Sixth Street in New York? How many times had I walked down this street with blood on my clothes from the cut-off end of a finger, with groceries in my arms for a dinner with friends, with a new man at my side for a night's work? How many times had I walked down East Sixth looking for sex? Or Indian food? Or both?

(Tim pulls his pants up, shimmying the whole way.)

Sometimes I would sit afterward in an Indian restaurant, beloved Kismoth or tasty Shagorika, snuggled into a booth with a man I was seeing. The cum would be still marking our bodies, crackly on my neck or sticky between his legs. The Bengali waiter would arrive with his freshly-starched-white-shirt smile.

Waiter, I'll have the mango chutney and a large Wash'n Dri, please.

How many footsteps have walked here before me, the memory of their soles wearing that East Village concrete into sand and dust? How many footprints of the dead who came before us are layered beneath our striding feet? Right now I might be stepping on the tiny footprints of Doug's dead grandma. I can follow her path as she walked up to Fourteenth Street from Delancey in 1912. She walked uptown to buy a book or a piece of meat. Maybe she was window-shopping for a dress she'd never be able to afford for the new year.

Our feet joined that throng.

Am I being sentimental here? Well, I'm sorry, but I listen to doomy and gloomy music frequently and this makes me remember the footfalls of the dead. I hear that music loud in my head. I do what it takes to keep the memory alive of each slaughtered queer poet on each battlefield or immune suppression ward. I remember every dyke and every faggot erased by this culture. I spend hours looking at the photos of my dead lovers on my altar at home. I touch my first SILENCE = DEATH button with a nostalgia I can't help but feel for 1988, my first tour of duty with ACT UP. I jab that SILENCE=DEATH pin into the palm of my hand. I hope for blood. I hope that the blood might actually mean something.

The light . . .

(Right on cue, a fierce diagonal of light bisects the stage.)

. . . pours in.

I had met him earlier that day, this man I'm walking with down East Sixth Street. We had become acquainted at Performance Space 122 during a gay men's performance workshop I was leading. The light had poured in PS 122's tall windows as I opened the curtains and swabbed the deck to get the room ready for the workshop. One by one the two dozen guys arrived, bundled up against the even-for-December cold. We gathered to tell some stories about our lives. I hoped the warm breath of our raised voices would keep us toasty. The weak 4 P.M. sun spread long and low on the floor as it shone through the somber stained-glass window that had preached to generations of immigrants this inscribed poem:

Every waking hour we weave,
whether we will or no—
Every trivial act or deed,
into the warp must go.

That "party on" message spread its soft glow on the group of huddled-together faggots eleven years into the plague. Arms around each other's shoulders sweaty and swaying. We're close enough to smell each other. We're close enough to listen to each other as our stories weave together. I look for these circles. Conjure them, too, sometimes.

"I'm Andrew," he had said as we went around sharing our names. This was the man I would walk down East Sixth Street with later that night. Andrew was broodingly dark and handsome, a Heathcliff on Houston kind of thing.

I know you, I thought to myself.

Andrew and I rose to our feet even as the workshop's tales of sissy boys and first loves swirled about us. I looked at him, and he met my gaze. Andrew and I were wearing almost exactly the same outfits (how unusual). We were boldly duochrome in our beat-up black sweatpants and white sleeveless T-shirts with crosses and religious medals dangling from our necks, sort of a City Ballet meets Saint Mark's Place kind of look. It was like we had spoken on the phone to decide what to wear to the first day of East Village High School!

"How long have you two known each other?" someone asked me, commenting on our similar getups.

"Not long enough," I whispered to myself as I maneuvered my way nearer to him. He was pretty big! Tall, I mean, a bit taller than me. I hated that. It meant that if we kissed later, I would have to twist my neck up and around to reach him. I would be sure to get a neck ache. I should probably just call my chiropractor right now and make an appointment. Andrew wore a religious medal I didn't immediately recognize. What was it? A petite Saint Peter and Saint Paul medal. Understated yet boner-producing.

Who was Andrew, anyway? His dark eyes and black hair reeled me right in. I could fight that tight fish line, try to get that hook out of the soft flesh of my cheek, but I knew the story would end up with me flopping around on the deck.

We snuck a look again, longer this time. What happens when these eyes meet? How can we fulfill the promise of that connection? How to receive it like an orange held in an open palm toward you? Well, there's all kinds of things you can do, of course. You can linger near each other, nearer than normal. You can yawn and extend your arm over the back of the chair. You can do this in your seats right now. You can ask each other silly questions like "Got the time? How about a light? Want some tea?" But when we feel the sacred buzz of this connection rise up from the earth, why can't we just go right up and say, "Hello Human, I am me! Who you are?" Why not? Why can't we do that? Is there a law or something? Do something. Cross that line. Take the scariest chance and seize the slippery day. Whatever it takes. DO IT! Like your life depends on it. Which it does.

Well, Andrew and I opted for the "linger near each other" approach. It's low-risk but also definitely low-yield. The workshop ended after three hours of creating performances about the secret powers we held as gay men; PS 122 was bursting with metaphors and hormones. Andrew and I hung around the room till almost all the participants had already left. We stood by our shoes, which had ended up next to each other (oh, fate!) on a well-worn seating platform. Those black boots waited for us to get our act together. They engaged in Doc Martens gossip.

The size ten and a half wide muttered, "I just wish they'd go talk to each other."

"I just wish they'd go fuck each other!" the eleven narrow complained through the sock that was suffocating him.

Finally, to shut the boots up before they said something really embarrassing, Andrew and I grabbed those Doc Martens and stuck our feet in their mouths and flattened their shoe tongues as we threaded every last eyelet. These were the eleven-hole, *not* the eight-hole variety, so this trying activity took a little while. Each diving swoop of those shoelaces drew Andrew and me nearer and nearer. Face-to-face while we waited for the last person to leave, we tugged the laces tight and made a knot. Everyone was now gone. One of us had to do something quick. I crossed my fingers and stepped into the void.

"Um, would you like to hang out for a while?"

"Sure," Andrew replied. "That would be great."

"What shall we do?"

"What would you like to do?" Andrew tossed it back to me.

"No, you decide," I countered.

"No, you," Andrew parried.

"It's up to you," I said almost shouting.

"You're the visitor in New York, it's definitely your decision," Andrew said, putting his Doc Martened foot down. Checkmate.

I wanted to say something like, "Let's just find a place that is quiet to sit and recognize the essential truth and spirit in each other." Because that is really what I hoped would happen. In lieu of that, I floated a more conventional proposal: "Why don't we go to Yaffa Cafe and eat something?"

Wrapping our Bob Cratchit scarves around our necks, we pushed our way out of the big oak doors of PS 122 and into the flow of the pre-Christmas jostle of First Avenue.

"It's fucking cold!" I complained, feeling like my lips were going to fall off with frostbite.

"Let's run," Andrew said and took off.

We quickly covered the short distance to the cafe, shoved through the crush in the narrow entry, and slipped into a cozy, warm corner table.

"I hate the winter," I, the typical Californian, complained. "I think it's why I left New York for California."

"Hey, I'm a Californian too," Andrew said, removing several layers of jackets and sweaters.

"You're kidding! Where are you from?" I was pleased to have discovered our common origin.

"Well," Andrew began, lavishing several vowels on this one word, as though this were a huge tale to tell, "I was born in Stockton in a manger, then when I was six . . ."

We were off and running in the delicious orgy of two native Californians comparing their tan lines as we shared nostalgic memories of hitchhiking in the San Joaquin Valley and which sex acts we had had on which rides at Disneyland.

We had tea surrounded by the late-baroque punk splendor of Yaffa on Saint Mark's. For two hours we talked and traded and teased and tempted as we lunged our pita bread into the spicy humus dip. Feeling daring, I licked the last bit up off the plate with my tongue and winked. This could have been the opening salvo of our intimacy, but Andrew glanced down at his watch.

"Oh, look at the time!" he said getting up. "I have to go to work. I'm late."

"Yikes!" I exclaimed, using a characteristic retro expression that made me sound like one of the Hardy Boys. "I have a show to do. I need to go too." Then I added nervously, "Would you like to meet later?"

"Sure," Andrew shouted through the pullover sweater that covered his face as he climbed into it. "This time I'll decide where to eat."

Later that night, at 10 P.M., I walked down First Avenue feeling pretty good. I was addicted to the feeling of excitement that came from having a rendezvous scheduled with God Knows Who to do God Knows What with each other. I walked down the avenue. Past Holy Stromboli Pre-Lubricated Pizza. Past the sour-cream-filled pleasures of Poland and the Ukraine. I went into a restaurant at East Sixth Street and Avenue A where Andrew and I were to meet. It was called Banditos or Caballeros or something like that.

I looked around the restaurant for Andrew. I couldn't see a sign of him. *I've been abandoned!* I thought to myself as I turned into a puddle of panic. Then I saw Andrew waving madly, trying to get my attention from the little table behind the pillar. Counting my breaths in an effort to calm my involuntary hyperventilating, I lugged my "abandonment issues" in their enormous mismatched steamer trunks across the restaurant and sat down across from him.

"Hi!" Andrew said as he leaned across the table and gave me a matter-of-fact kiss.

"Hi," I replied. One breath. Two breaths. Three breaths. "Nice to see you. Have you been waiting long?"

"Nah. Long enough to order a margarita. Are you okay?"

"Oh, sure, I'm fine." I improvised nonchalance, kicking the panic-filled steamer trunks further under the table till they fit. "I just got a little nervous as I walked here."

"Relax." Andrew rubbed my forearm. "I won't bite."

The margarita arrived: a frosty tureen the size of a bassinet. The salt chunks trembled in slow motion down the melting sides.

"Waiter," Andrew asked, "can we have two straws?"

Nursing our beverage, Andrew and I swapped stories of love and families and school and coming out and hopes and fears. In other words, we had a conversation. The stories bounced back and forth like a first round of tennis between a couple of people getting to know each other's skill. Our game plan included the usual dinner conversation topics: hustler boyfriends, drama queenism, international travel, and adolescent erotics.

"I had a boyfriend once who was a hustler on Santa Monica Boulevard," I started with an easy overhand serve. "He told me he did it so that he could buy a grand piano. But after all those blow jobs, once he got that grand piano, he found he could only play in E minor."

Andrew returned the lob with a free association: "Well, now that you mention blow jobs and the performing arts, I got my first blow job at the International Thespian Conference in Muncie, Indiana. It was with a boy from St. Cloud, Wisconsin, and happened backstage during a parochial girls' school production of *You Can't Take It with You*."

Lunging to display my backhand, I sent the ball back with a difficult corner shot. "Oh, yes, travel brings out the best in us. My friend Doug and I once had a big fight in the Parc Royal in Brussels, so we split up for a couple of days and then met to the train station in Berlin Bahnhofzoo. We saw each other next to the express train to Moscow. Doug and I were so happy to see each other as we hugged and kissed our way onto the U-Bahn that we almost missed our stop at Karl Marx Platz."

Andrew was good, very good; he stretched long and thwacked the ball into my court with a story that psyched me out: "When I was seventeen, I lived with my mom in a house in the San Joaquin Valley next to some alfalfa fields. Every night of my seventeenth year, I walked far out into those fields. I would carefully take off all of my clothes and then jerk off over those green alfalfa leaves, dreaming of the Latino workers of those fields."

I reached for the ball but missed. Game and match!

The edgy cultural politics of this alfalfa field story had given me an instant hard-on. "Waiter, can we have the check, please? Por favor?"

Andrew and I quickly paid the bill. Finally, our bodies brushed together as we walked down East Sixth Street in the direction of his house on this cold night in New York City.

We strolled past the mysterious fort-like walls of the Con Edison electrical plant at Sixth Street and Avenue A. It looked like a Wild West outpost for some minor John Wayne movie. The sides of our bodies moved closer yet as we wandered past the bright facade of my favorite gay watering hole, the Wonder Bar. The hopeful primary colors were as brilliant as my third-grade Jonny Quest lunch box. We walked on and on toward Avenue B.

(Tim walks toward someone in the front row and addresses them.)

Now, you're probably saying to yourself, "My God, Tim does go on about meeting men!" Well, that's true. I'm guilty as charged. But I do this because I believe these connections are a great gift and secret adventure of life. It's like the prize at the bottom of the Cracker Jack box. You dig way beyond the sticky stuff, the bodies, the sex even, and there at the bottom *is* the magic decoder ring! It can help us understand the world and how we move through it. It's like a doorway that opens. A window creaks up through all the layers of paint and opens over our hearts. And maybe only one moment of every year, the dawn sunrise on winter solstice maybe, can the light shine all the way to the back to the darkest place inside us.

And at that exact moment, one human being can dare to ask the other, "Do you wanna come in?"

OOOOOOHHH! What a question! It's the question of our time. In these lives are a meeting at the corner of East Sixth and Avenue B.

We got to Andrew's building. Was this the building in which I built a loft bed for that New York University film student who then bounced his Citibank check on me?

Andrew asked me, "Do you wanna come in?"

I wish that life were that simple, that tidy. This wasn't how it happened at all. Andrew didn't ask me. I had to ask *him*.

"Gee," I enthused, channeling Joe Hardy this time, "here we are at your house. Can I come in?" What a cad! But I dared to take a chance.

"Oh, sure," Andrew said, pleased but a little surprised.

We went up the narrow stairs. Up, up, up into his apartment. Andrew struggled heroically with the police lock, the dead bolt, and the door-handle lock (part of the nonstop glamour of New York living), and we tumbled into the dark apartment. No one else seemed to be home. That was good, I thought to myself. The solitude would make the preliminary moves toward grabbing each other's bodies more smooth. No distracting conversations *à trois* in the kitchen.

Andrew began to show me his sacred things, the apartment relics and icons. He had his extracted wisdom teeth placed on the altar next to the TV. His barbells stacked next to the radiator by the shelves with the hand-painted ceramic dinosaur collection ordered from the Franklin Mint. Three Virgin Marys on the toilet tank.

Finally, Andrew tugged me into his whitewashed bedroom to see a sixth-grade class photo. I was dismayed to notice his bed, a beat-up old futon, in one corner *on the floor*! I couldn't stop myself from beginning to redesign Andrew's bedroom. I had a

vision of how this room would benefit from one of my loft beds. I saw where I would put it on the wall, bolting the bed frame to the wall halfway up on the window, keeping the light above and below. Drawing the plans in my head, I imagined how this would open up an area underneath for a desk or a love seat.

For now, we flopped down on his futon on the floor, and I admired his black, black, black hair against the bed's white, white, white sheet. With a studied casualness I flopped one of my legs over one of Andrew's as we stared up at the ceiling in an uncomfortable what-will-happen-next? silence. Andrew and I now faced that most challenging of existential situations: Who is going to make the first move?

Before we mere humans could answer, Andrew's pet feline, Hamster the Miracle Cat, poked into the room. Hamster the Miracle Cat probably was really on the lookout for some extra wet food from that morning's still-open cat food can on the roach-friendly kitchen counter. But, meanwhile, Hamster proceeded to perform the "cat head thing," when a cat drops all pretense of aloofness and caresses you with its entire face. I suppose the animal kingdom was daring us to be more spontaneous and find our touch together. By example, Hamster tried to teach us how to rub the head into the crotch and drag our body's side against another body's side.

Taking the lead from Hamster, Andrew and I began to rub our faces together. The tip of my nose caressed Andrew's cheek as his lips grazed over my stubble closer to my open mouth. We kissed.

Oh, I liked Andrew. He was kind and smart and hot and he was a Californian like me, yet he wore even more black clothes than I did! We savored taking those black clothes off—hands reaching into the 501's, tugging down the thick sweat socks, yawning out of our shirts with a sigh. The thrill of each touch given and received made my thoughts tumble in my head like clothes in a dryer.

Wow, I thought to myself as my hands searched Andrew's skin. *His leg goes into his hip right there. Unheard of! He has a little hair here on his belly but not here on his shoulders. Fantastic! His recently shaved balls are attached to his dick in a bouncy sack-like structure. Wonder of wonders! The skin is so soft. His mouth tastes good. This all feels good.*

I sensed Andrew's ceramic dinosaur collection beginning to stir from the shelf above. The prehistoric creatures slowly levitated above us as we licked each other's cocks. One ceramic Virgin Mary statue floated in just to bless us as we got closer. All of Andrew's childhood snapshots sneaked out of the drawer where they had been stashed. The photos set up a camp around the bed, the past witnessing this present moment. Even his barbells started to move a little nearer to each other and, at last, began to clang together as well.

Well, to make a long story short, I came on his chest. He came on my leg. I was glad I was there. I was glad I was alive. I loved New York. This was too good. Something bad was bound to happen. With that doom-laden thought, I fell into a deep sleep full of nightmares of exploding buildings and machine-gunned nuns.

The next morning we woke up early in the flashbulb-bright sunshine coming in from the East River. I was covered in that sticky-cum-closeness of waking up with someone for the first time. I felt the splurge of feelings that can happen as you wake up in bed with another human. One or two of my masks came down: scary, even though there were still lots held in reserve. Turning tentatively onto my side, I looked to Andrew to see if he was awake. His eyes were open but still sleepy.

"Hi, handsome," Andrew tossed my way.

"Good morning." I yawned out the words as I stretched. "Do you mind morning mouth?"

Andrew kissed by way of reply. We were tentative about opening our mouths to each other, like checking the milk with a sniff after you've been away from home for a few days. The morning kiss floated on the grace of trusting that we liked each other, and neither one of us was going to make a hasty exit.

"So," Andrew said, beginning the cross-examination as he abruptly broke off the kiss, "you probably have a boyfriend, right?"

"Yeah." I opted for a matter-of-fact tone. "We've been together ten years this month. His name is Doug. We have an open relationship."

"If I were him," Andrew said, rubbing his knuckles playfully, though a little roughly, on my forehead, "I wouldn't let you wander around without a chaperon."

Andrew and I lounged as we talked shop about boyfriends, present and past. I could slowly see our conversation was inevitably going to come around to *the* subject, the AIDS tune-in.

Now, at that time in my life, I usually didn't engage in this conversation on the first date. Being a good ACT UP boy, I assumed all my partners were positive and behaved accordingly. Normally, I would wait and have the HIV talk after I had sex with a fellow a couple of times. I don't think I'm alone in this. Let's see a show of hands.

(Tim scans the audience.)

I did this because I believe in safe sex. I believe in safe sex and its principles. I structure my life around its precepts. I have to believe in safe sex just like I have to believe in other forces essential for life: gravity, photosynthesis, friction. This faith allows me to get up in the morning, make my breakfast, and *not* have a nervous breakdown. I do believe in safe sex, I do I do I do!

Since Andrew and I had been careful—RESPECTFUL—in our sex, according to the accepted mores of the time, this was a perfectly responsible time to have the discussion, if indeed we even needed to have it. The subject came up on its own, as it so often does.

I said, "Andrew, it's intense to be here, lying in a bed on East Sixth Street, talking about all this relationship material. My boyfriend John that I told you about, who died of AIDS, he used to live on East Sixth, just down the block."

"Ouch," Andrew said, hugging his arms around me. We breathed together for a bit. "It sucks, I know. My ex-boyfriend back in California is pretty sick right now. I worry about him a lot."

We held this close between us.

"So, Andrew . . . um . . ." I hemmed and hawed, trying to spit out the obvious question. "Where are you in all of this AIDS stuff?"

"I'm positive," Andrew said, looking directly at me. "I just found out a little while ago. What about you?"

"I'm negative. The one time I checked anyway. I could hardly believe it, considering my history. You know . . . John and all."

Well, the cards were on the table: It was a full house. The cameras zoomed in for the close-up. Everything was going real slow, spooky and sci-fi. At this point there was a hydrogen bomb blast over the East River. This explosion blared through the windows onto our bodies, burning away the bullshit between Andrew and me. I witnessed a powerful moment between two human faggots at the end of the twentieth century.

I felt as if a strange bird, strange as the subject at hand, had flown into Andrew's bedroom. This creature was a little clumsy, awkward as Big Bird, as it broke through the glass and flapped around Andrew's room, knocking his high school graduation pictures off of the wall. This bird landed there at the end of Andrew's futon and looked at us. This bird, like this moment between us, could be fierce or friendly. It was *totally* up to us.

I looked Andrew in the eye. I had nothing useful to say, nothing that wouldn't collapse under the weight of its own structure of obvious verbs and insufficient adjectives. I felt our fates float around us for a moment. There was a hurt that hovered over Andrew's face for an even tinier instant.

"I hope you're not freaked out that I didn't tell you earlier," Andrew said quietly, looking down toward our feet.

"No." I said the right thing, though I knew no single word could describe the snarl of feelings that were revving up inside. Without thinking, I quickly toured the inside of my mouth with my tongue to see if I had any canker sores there. Everything seemed okay. "I'm a big boy. I know how to take care of myself."

Then, I put my lips on Andrew's. Our tongues touched, and it was like a promise, eyes open, hearts too. Andrew and I started to make love again. We moved our hands over the hills and valleys of our bodies just as we had a few hours before. I felt a powerful mix of excitement and fear. What was different now? There was an honest thrill in knowing who we really were.

I knew something special had happened. I didn't want to make it into a big deal. In a way it was just how things were, our lives as we needed to live them. I wasn't even sure what any of this positive/negative information meant anymore. But if I tried to say it meant *nothing* to me at that moment, that would have been a lie, a whopper of a lie. I was so tired of lying.

I had been in this situation before, of course, with other men who were positive. There was that time with the guy from Cedar Rapids. Or the fellow from Spokane. One man was white. Another man was black. I confess they were all cute. All dear. All very hot. I am weak.

One of these men used to lead workshops in Texas for ex-gay born-again Christians. That didn't last too long before he met a nice boy at a gay bar in Tulsa. They moved to San Francisco, and he now works in a card shop in the Castro.

Another man won a scholarship to Princeton where he pored over medieval texts while eyeing the water polo players with his feet propped up on the back of the swimming arena bleachers.

One man escaped the death squads in San Salvador and walked all the way through Guatemala and Mexico to make a new life in Los Angeles. He sent money each week to his family.

Another man went home with Jeffrey Dahmer yet managed to live and tell the tale. (If that's not a fucking success story, I don't know what is.)

All of these men were positive. They told me this. They knew. I'm negative. I was pretty surprised that the coin flipped that way. It always scares me to tell people this. I worry that they'll think I'm a lightweight-know-nothing-who-said-you-could-talk-about-AIDS-from-your-position-of-negative-privilege queen.

I put my skin next to the skin of each of these men. I needed their touch, maybe more than they needed mine. I loved one man's crazy Brillo hair, his crooked smile, his deeply dimpled ass. I loved another man's wild courage at his job, his scary family story, his dick that veered to the left like a stretch of road.

What's "safe" anyway in this crazy life? Not getting out of bed, that might be safe. Except, I live in California where an earthquake might drop your house on you while you slept. Not crossing against traffic and getting hit by a delivery truck like I almost did on the way to the theater tonight. Not climbing on slippery rocks, which I simply must do every day at my beach in Venice. Not ever getting close, close enough to touch.

Oh, but this kiss, I gotta have it. It's that simple. I gotta have it if my friend allows it to me. I can't stand on one side of a stupid river and wave a clumsy oar. No. I need this kiss and I want to know its *whole* story. I worry sometimes. I get scared. In my life that is too much ruled by fear. I fear everything. Earthquakes. Plane crashes. My face in the mirror. I get scared I'll trip on this crack on the stage and break my leg. But I have a special wing of fear, about the size of the Louvre, dedicated to the things that I might "get" from the men I get close to. Do sex with.

(Over the sound system we hear the scary whine of an electric planer, redolent of that day in Brooklyn.)

CLAP! WARTS! HEPATITIS! CRABS! AMOEBAS! HIV! This fear chews me up for breakfast. This fear is a tidal wave that is hovering above me, whirling, threatening. My mouth frozen in a scream. This fear is a virus too. It's a fierce enemy, takes no prisoners. Can haunt my dreams. After some sex that, okay, wasn't so safe, it keeps me sleepless and tortured at 3 A.M.

in South Kensington, London. Spitting distance from the gloriously tacky memorial to Prince Albert, who long before he was a dick piercing, was the beloved of Victoria. When Albert died, Victoria (that queen) took whatever was good and hot in her and entombed it with Albert, her dead husband, and worshipped them all as dead things!

Lately, I've tried to turn this fear around. To flip that word "get" upside down. Like a fried egg. Over. Easy. To see things another way. I want to honor the things that I actually "get" from other men.

LOVE. TOUCH. INSPIRATION. SEX. KISSES AND WISDOM.

These are the things I get and give and get again. Just like I'm getting from my new friend, Andrew, on East Sixth Street. I want to kiss him. To feel his wet, wet, wet tongue. To feel our hearts grow with us together. To feel the way this sex pulls us somewhere good even while the frozen wind howls over the scary water towers of Grammercy Park and tomorrow morning, after the blizzard of the century, there will be absolutely *no* subway service to Brooklyn.

"Wait. Wait. Wait. Wait!" I hear a voice in my head say. *"I paid my twelve dollars. Isn't it about time something BAD happened to these guys? Toward the end of the show, it's the agreed-upon time. Shouldn't one of them get sick and die now? You made your bed Mr. Fag Carpenter. Now lie in it! Or maybe somebody could come in with a chain saw and cut some stuff off, splatter those white walls with red blood. God needs his pound of flesh!"* This voice says to me, *"You don't deserve this pleasure."*

Sorry. Nothing so dramatic tonight, nothing so tragic. I hope you're not disappointed. Andrew and I became friends. Made love a bunch of times. Once, even, in Annie Sprinkle's sacred bed next to the crystal dildo collection. We have swum in each other's oceans. Santa Monica. Coney Island. Seen each other with other men. Run up high phone bills between New York and LA.

Another big cost of intimacy. We have been in life together. And that's a pretty good story.

But like in every story something did happen that December in 1992. Andrew and I knelt in a circle, our knees to the earth, cocks in each other's hands. Can anybody here tonight really see those positive and negative signs hovering over our heads? I can't. But I could feel the electricity we were generating. I felt the juice come up through the floors of the tenement on East Sixth Street. I felt this buzz come up from the earth and move through me. I could feel it, the actual conjure of this thing.

Maybe in that circle of dicks and tongues and the past and the future we can throw a mess of slippery K-Y-covered marbles in front of those four cranky dudes on horseback as they pound down the streets inside each of us.

Maybe we can smack those jaws of fate and grab a shiny gold cock ring from that creaky dental work and slip it on.

Maybe our laughs and brave chests and saucy attitudes can find the punch line and the way out.

Maybe as I dangled my cross around my neck on its bathtub chain into Andrew's open mouth I'll find some answers.

Maybe as Andrew leaned over and pinched my tit and dropped his Saint Peter and Saint Paul medal between my lips and it fell deep inside me we'll learn something important. We'll get our hooks into each other, fishing for some truth or at least a gasp and a squirt. Testing and tasting each other's metal. Catching good things and not throwing them away waiting for something bigger and better.

Andrew came on his belly and chest and then so did I. I leaned over him and kissed him as I dragged this cross on this bathtub chain through that cum. Mixing it up. Now, no chemistry class ever taught me this experiment. I had to learn it myself. How to find the alchemy to mix this stuff up into something neither this nor that. Neither only him nor only me.

What do we do from this maybe knowing that maybe one of us will maybe die before the other maybe and in a fashion we

know too well for sure? Well, we better have that fuel us and focus us cause we got work to do. Cause that cross belongs in our mouths. It should be moved from tongue to tongue and taste to taste. I pulled it from between Andrew's teeth with a clank and my cock was in a rubber in his ass and there was only yes and pleasure and it's one small step for man one giant leap for homokind and we'll plant that flag wherever we choose but always looking for the proper soil and ready to sing the needed psalm.

Then . . . we came again. It's nice when it works. It's like a handshake. A tip of the hat. A thin rubber skin between us. A contract.

Then we had the ultimate ritual. We walked naked to Andrew's dark kitchen, opened the fridge, and there—by the soft light of Amana—we drank some orange juice from the bottle.

> *(The sound of waves at the ocean slowly washes over the theater. Over the sound of the sea, we hear some delicate and more-than-a-little-melancholy music. The lights pull close and blue around Tim.)*

Then we slept. The deep breath of sleep. Faces next to each other. Breath swapping. Atoms dancing around each other. And I dreamed. I dreamed I had built a bed. I'd found my tools and I'd built a fine bed that was floating on the sea. It was a seaworthy bed! And my friend and I were sailing toward a safe harbor. I dreamed of that bed on the sea. Of beautiful trees on the shore. Graceful gestures between humans. And good bread that had been baked for us to eat in the morning at our leisure.

What if we were looking at *this* scene from outer space. Oh. God. What a thing to see. It's a beautiful sight. We would see many men, many people floating on their beds at sea, dreaming *their* dreams. Reaching for the touch, the best part of ourselves.

We would see how those men had once been little boys who cried too much before Sunday school. Or dressed up too much in their mom's clothes. Or touched themselves too much under the covers at night. And needed other boys . . . just enough.

From outer space it would seem that Earth is a very strange planet 'cause people made war upon these boys. Priest and parents and politicians teased them and tortured them. So, these boys learned to run fast. Maybe too fast. Some of you are here tonight.

They learned how to find each other. On the street and in Laundromats. Construction sites and theaters. This is a very good story. It's a story we should tell again and again. It's that magic decoder ring given to us as our birthright, at the same time as we got our black leather jackets and superior sense of humor. We queer people made a place for ourselves. Cooked the meal. Made the bed. Waved that red shirt above our naked bodies. Dared to ask each other "Do you wanna come in?"

For a while, things were pretty good. Well, okay, they weren't that good. But they were better than they'd been in seventh grade at Andrew Jackson Junior High in Fruitland, New Mexico. From outer space we would see that a great plague fell upon these beds at sea. And of these boys who had become men, fine men, many had fallen. And the ones who still breathed felt a cold place. It hurt so bad. A frozen tear. A tear inside. A wound that would numb us. Stop us. Cut us. Hurt us.

From outer space we would see that these brave people found many ways through this hard time.

They found ways to keep dancing that dance. Holding each other. Caring for each other.

Finding each other. In Laundromats. Construction sites. Theaters . . . and on the street.

We all have a street inside us. A place where some things happened. Some wounds opened. Others healed. Food was eaten. Losses mourned. I am a carpenter. And I will build a bed. I'll build a place inside myself to honor my friends, my journey, and the streets I've strolled. As I live and breathe. In. And out. In. And out.

(Lights begin very slow fade to black.)

And with this breath I will draw us close.
Wrap you all around me.
Float on your SIGH . . .
As these lights . . .
slowly . . .
fade.

Fruit Cocktail

I cooked up *Fruit Cocktail* in 1995 because I had just fallen in love and was ready for a break. Finally giving myself a much-needed furlough from the AIDS and culture wars—vacations come hard for WASPs—I wanted to focus on a sweet and fun story I had never told. What I was going to do on my art holiday was explore the twenty-four hour period in 1976 during which I turned eighteen, came out to my parents, and had sex for the very first time.

For a dozen years of performance making I had been at such a high pitch of committing my creative work to the crisis du jour. In each show I stepped up to the plate to address Reagan's election or the nuclear war panic or the AIDS crisis or the NEA controversy or the negotiation of psychological and sexual space for gay men in the nineties. I almost didn't know what it would be like to make such a sweet show! Was I being mellowed by the narcotic haze of the relatively homo-friendly Clinton administration and the early glimpses of the AIDS cocktail arriving on the horizon? What was I to do? The set is not decorated with demonic Republicans lurking stage left! No untimely deaths of lovers or friends! No untangling of garden-variety (perennial, that is) systemic homophobia! What a fucking relief! What I was left with was the joyous potential and pleasure of my first love, first sex, and coming out/into self. This performance was such pleasure to perform.

Strange that of all the autobiographical narratives I had recounted in my shows I had never told the Gay 101 story: COMING OUT. Patrick Merla had asked me to write such a story for a collection he was editing for Avon Books called *Boys Like Us*. I quickly saw that I wanted to play with the writing and explore its performance possibilities. Maybe the fact that I had fallen in love the year before also had something to do with this more vernal and chipper space I was exploring. I had met Alistair McCartney in London in 1994 and gone head-over-heels. During the next two years I was involved in a very difficult and emotionally challenging breakup with my partner of thirteen years, Doug Sadownick. When *Fruit Cocktail* premiered in 1996, my life was beginning to take a new shape, groaning and heaving and shifting with big tectonic forces. In a strange way I was feeling quite close to that adolescent self, all tortured and idealistic and ready to change.

In spite of the roiling offstage personal dramas, I am almost chagrined at how bushy-tailed this work is. Capacious—a word I even allow myself to use in the performance—in its adolescent *joie de sex, Fruit Cocktail* imagines a queer coming of age moment that is remarkably free of angst and angina. Wish fulfillment? A little bit, maybe, but true to what that precise late-seventies moment felt like to me. It was the rich fuel that would fling me to New York at the age of nineteen to begin creating my work.

Indeed, all the performances contained in this volume are fueled by gay love and eros; they are tributes to the gifts men can bring one another. Call me a relationship junkie, but I believe the charting of these homo love narratives has been one of my biggest jobs as an artist. While making *Fruit Cocktail,* I was being transformed by what I was going through with Doug and Alistair. This seemed like the perfect moment to create a performance to honor my first lover, David, who brought me to a most juicy fruition.

In addition to being a thank-you note to the first love-of-my-life, the show also tips the hat to the other muses that helped me on my way. *Fruit Cocktail* constellates (germinates?) around the Cal State University, Fullerton, dance studio where I would meet David and eventually make love for the first time. This gives me an excuse to acknowledge the ways that dance saved my life. Getting to escape from the horrors of PE in high school by taking a modern dance class allowed me to connect with my changing body/desires and gave me a runway that made all my future performance work possible. The show also has one of my favorite uses of juicy, overblown music with my pop-your-cherry monologue set to the "Amen" from Handel's *Messiah*. I make frequent inspiration pit stops in my performances to the canonical classical music literature: Copland's *Appalachian Spring*, Ravel's *Bolero*, Wagner's *Liebestod*, Beethoven's Ninth Symphony. I go to the top of the charts! This was the music that inflated my self-importance, got me hard, and catapulted me to imagine that my little life mattered. Whether it was the power of dance, Handel's *Messiah*, or a PBS play about Oscar Wilde, all of these cultural materials provided me a primer on queer agency and a road map for identity.

I was thirty-six when I wrote *Fruit Cocktail*, in 1995. It indulges a sunny memory of a moment eighteen years before. It occupies a liminal space, a warm patch of sun between the Reagan/Bush/AIDS era and the new storm looming on the horizon for my relationship with Alistair in this country where we have no rights. But for a couple of years during the creation and touring of this show, it was good to remember the feisty and fierce love of my eighteenth year and to feel its heat and ongoing challenge to me now, that potential to grow and change. *Fruit Cocktail* returns us to my Whittier backyard, that primal psychic-cum-suburban launching pad surrounded by orange trees. This is the story of how to grow fruit!

(The stage is set, festooned even, with painted orange tree branches and a tall row of punky spiked bright green grass bordering the upstage wall. There is a homocentric, ancient Greek, Corinthian pillar upstage right with a galvanized bucket sitting on top. On a good night we hope the set's effect is both formal and saucy. Tim enters with branches, doing the fruit dance. He enjoys this for a while and then notices the audience.)

Hi, everybody. This is my "fruit dance." I've been taking some workshops at the Center for Integral Fruition here in Santa Monica. We're exploring our corporeal meditations to connect to one's Fruit Guide within. I know you're mostly lay people here tonight, so it might seem a little confusing. Let me explain what I'm doing with this fruit dance. You probably saw me doing this brushing movement. This brings all the energy in the space toward me. It goes right up to the genital chakra. Then to the heart chakra and back to you. It's an ecology, the great circle of life.

In what my dance friends see as the most dynamic shift in this fruit meditation, we see this stamping motion followed by a lateral gesture. This brings into my spirit the possibility of rooting and budding.

Everyone recognizes this visceral series of whipping motions. Now, as you all know, in many world religions, and in all leather clubs, whipping is used as a way of altering consciousness. In this case, this whipping reminds me of the pain, for there is pain involved in that tender little bud breaking through the hard bark.

Finally, in this most integrated sequence, this sacred series of movements connects head and dick, head and dick. You may have to do this one for a while. It's followed by a big sweeping mid-seventies modern dance movement. This shows my commitment

to nurturing my queer fruit within. I'll do the whole thing so you get the organic flow.

(Tim does dance once more with feeling.)

It works for me.

This is not new for me. I've been working with fruit for a long time. In kindergarten, they gave us each an apple sapling. We planted them out next to the jungle gym on Whittier Boulevard. They showed my kindergarten class the Disney Johnny Appleseed cartoon on a daily basis. We would sing the Johnny Appleseed hit single, "For giving me the things I need, the sun and the rain and an apple seed (sing along everyone), the Lord is good to me!"

My first-grade teacher Mrs. Walters was good to me too ("teacher's pet") cause she gave me two apple saplings. ("Because you're such a special, though unusual, boy.") As those tiny apple trees grew, I saw that magic was possible. It existed as concretely as the fourteen layers of hair spray on Mrs. Walters's hurricane-gale-resistant bouffant existed.

Those saplings grew and so did I. They are tall trees today. Years later, another teacher in the California public school system continued the fruit lesson with the old Avocado, Toothpick, Glass of Water trick.

(Tim peers into a bucket. Light reflects off a mirror in the bottom and shines up onto his face.)

That avocado seed stripped of its flesh, tortured with toothpicks, and perched there over the lure of that shimmering water (see, it's shimmering). My friend Ralph Higgs and I put our succulent twelve-year-old bodies very near each other as we stared at the reflection of our faces in that water. We wanted to see if that avocado seed was gonna crack through its shell and send its roots down toward that hot and wet place. Just as my love for Ralph was growing toward the heat and damp. The roots of that love as deep as the roots of the trees in the avocado groves where we walked every day after school, looking for arrowheads that didn't exist.

Ralph and I leaned over the first-peach-of-the-season-colored, protozoa-patterned Formica table. I was drunk with the nearness of his body. Ooooh. I wanted to reach underneath that untucked, mottled green Boy Scout shirt and let my fingers wander over his drum-taut belly and tiny nipples. I stood behind him and saw the smooth skin and downy hairs at the back of his neck. I reached forward to touch him but something stopped me. ("Shields up, Lieutenant Worf!") I tried to fight it and my hand moved closer. A tiny moan escaped from my lips. Ralph turned around and looked at me funny. He moved away and said, "I think we should go play war now."

In my backyard in Southern California, which is where the show is set, we had a number of fruit trees: lemon, persimmon, pomegranate, loquat. But there was one very special fruit tree, a Valencia orange. The one remaining tree of the orange grove that used to be there.

(Mysterious music fills the theater. A single orange flies down from above on a string.)

Somehow, as I grew up, that orange tree slowly became the symbol of my family. (This was a special hybrid tree bred to withstand the pressure of even the heaviest metaphor!) Every waking dream and unnamed desire dangled there as heavy as that fruit. I would lay underneath that tree naked when no one was home. I'd beg those branches to help me grow. I'd prick my finger on its sharp thorns and drip my blood into the dirt. C'mon, let's make a deal. I wanted its roots to wind through me and let me become part of the tree. I wanted to be as juicy and dangerously tart as the fruit of those Valencias. Those oranges so sour and sweet and sharp that one bite could make your face sphincter up into a Jesse Helms look-alike. Their juice would make you breathe your life in deep. I'd jerk off in the light of day when nobody was home

and cum on that tree root. I'd ask it for things they said no one should ask for.

(The orange goes back to where it came from, as long as the transparent fish line doesn't get tangled up like it did once in Atlanta.)

I'd try to actually see the tree grow. If I watched really closely with my child's eye, I was sure I could see it happen. I'd lay there very still and watch that orange against the sky. I'd see it oh so slowly grow beyond its boundaries.

Just like I tried to watch my pubic hair grow when I was a boy.

(House lights up. Time to torture the audience. Tim heads for the front row and picks on somebody.)

I need some help. Could you please pull one pubic hair out.

(Sometimes they resist pulling a pubic hair and Tim needs to encourage them a bit.)

Audience participation, ya gotta love it. Just pull the damn thing!!!

(Often they grab a handful. This is hard when there are eight shows a week.)

Ouch, you took too many; now I'm gonna need a pubic toupee! I waited such a long time for my first pubic hair. I was a late bloomer. I'd read all of Nietzsche and Schopenhauer twice before my voice began to change. Not a good idea. I was tired of being made fun of in the showers in gym class. I tried to *will* my pubic hair to grow. I'd concentrate very hard, "GROW GROW!" then I would get the flashlight and a mirror and then contort myself to see if anything was growing around my dick or butthole. When would I get my first pubic hair? I decided to take extreme action. I thought I could maybe help them grow. I would go out in the backyard and lay naked in the sun under the sprinklers when no one was home. No one was home a lot. The graceful arc of the water drenching me. Maybe my pubic hair had been planted with special pubic hair seed. Like the little specks on a poppyseed bagel. If I watered them they would grow. The sun might accelerate them. I sensed, as I looked at my hairless boy-belly and crotch, that when these hairs finally came they would bring some new revelation, a new awareness (ssss). I wanted this to happen soon. I started putting food supplements, house plant vitamins, fertilizers on my crotch to make that fucking pubic hair grow. In desperation, I even sent away for special miracle hair tonics for male pattern baldness. I was sure that would help. NADA!

Finally, one day, I saw something. I had just finished re-reading *Also Sprach Zarathustra*. Was it a speck of dirt? A bit of lint? No. It was an actual hair. I doubled up on the vitamin E oil and hot towel treatments. That pubic hair grew from an eighth of an inch to a quarter to a half an inch long. I got out my chemistry set microscope and saw there was some strange hieroglyphic writing on this first "naturally curly" pubic hair. I slowly deciphered the words on that pube.

(Tim reads the fine print on the pubic hair.)

"Greetings! Things will not be as you think. You are going to have a very different life from the other boys on your water polo team. You will want to hold and be held by other men. You will feel the tide of gender shift around inside of you. Sacred visions may appear. You will have an unusually developed appreciation for female vocalists of all eras. Welcome to your life."

End of message. This was my first pubic hair. There soon would be more and more. Each with its own tidings and greetings for the life to come. A forest of tales and guideposts for how to live my life.

As I look at you now, dear audience, I see you too as a lush field of pubic hair. Raise your arms and let that pubic hair dance. Each of you unique in your pubic splendor. C'mon do it. I promise you this is the most uncool moment in the show.

(Amazingly, the audience always does the arm wave. Tim works the room.)

This pubic hair suffers from K-Y buildup. This pube's gone gray. Lady Clairol'll fix that. All you not waving your arms must have a bad case of crabs. I'm going over here. Let those arms dance. Each of you pubic hairs here present has grown through many challenges and crises to be here tonight. You have grown up and through your bodies to get your butts on these seats tonight. Dance pubic arms. Dance. Woman or man. Straight or gay. Wait. One moment. Just for tonight I'm gonna assume everyone here tonight is queer. (I'm in a risk-taking mood.) For the three of you here tonight who are *not* queer, I'd like you to know that I'm empowered by the state of California to deputize you all right now. All you men, you're all cocksuckers and you've been up and down the Hershey Highway so much ya got enough frequent flyer miles for a round-trip to Cleveland. All you women, you are all clitlickers. If you're not queer, just see this as a compliment. It's kind of a mixture of what does daddy do at work and queen for a day.

Okay, lovely queer audience waving your pubic hair arms in this gentle breeze, how did we fulfill the promise and the prophecy of that pubic hair? How did we get through the gauntlet of a zillion cultural pressures to the contrary? Pulled this way and that. PULLED. Pulled as if by great ropes. Why look. Some rope. Got a date later. Grab these please. You people hold this end. You people this one.

(Tim gives the front row two ropes so they can tug him from side to side. The front row gets a real workout in this show!)

We were buffeted by the cold winds of cruel conformity— buffet me NOW please by the cold winds of cruel conformity . . . back and forth.

Fucked over by growing up in a homophobic world.

Messed with by right-wing homophobic hate-spewing.
The harsh challenge of AIDS.
The tyranny of conventional gender behavior!
(Build to a climax here, okay?)

(Before this gets out of hand Tim lets go of the ropes.)

Thanks for the buffeting.

I think I've always really known what finally got me through that shit and helped me be queer. It was written there in the really fine print on that pubic hair. I sense a TV signal tuning in. When you get right down to it, it all came down to one thing. PBS made me gay.

(Stage lights bright. Time to get down to business.)

Yes, here we have every right-wing nut's 3 A.M. nightmare come true. They broadcast that homo beam right into my family's suburban living room in the mid-seventies and saved my fucking life. It was that *Theater in America* production about Oscar Wilde. Thank you KCET! From you, public television, I received my first dose of queer images and a sense of historical lineage! (I got a tote bag too, but that's another story.) Well, maybe I can't give PBS *all* the credit. It could also have been that Civic Light Opera production in the late sixties of *A Funny Thing Happened on the Way to the Forum*. It was a notorious revival with the butt-revealing tunics on the chorus boys. Or, while we're in a Greco-Roman mood, maybe it was those delicious homoerotic novels by Mary Renault. (DYKE! WE LOVE YOU MARY!) Her books were set in classical Greece and were full of those buffed Athenian ephebes going for Truth and Beauty and Biceps. A little dab'll do ya! No, wait, I know. Wait! I know. It had to be the eighteenth-century composer George Frideric Handel. His music helped tell me who I was and sent me zooming into my queer life. Yes, there is absolutely no question (it's been scientifically proven)—Handel's *Messiah* made me into a faggot!

Allow me to explain. It is 1976. Ah, 1976! Let me smell the crotch of my maroon double-thick corduroy bell-bottoms and remember 1976! The capacious toothy grin of soon-to-be-President Jimmy Carter spreads like a shovel full of smooth peanut butter over the land. Let me take a whiff of Jif and sniff that tremulous year. Let me rub those bell-bottoms through my ass crack. Let me reach inside the pockets of those pants, past the tiny tube of Clearasil acne ointment, and grab my dripping teenage weenie.

I was seventeen going on eighteen and I was desperate for love and dick. I searched everywhere for it to no avail. During my entire sixteenth year, I constantly cruised the psychology section of the Whittier Public Library and not a single cute grad student tried to pick me up. So throughout the forty-years-in-the-desert of my adolescence, my backyard had been my only dependable sexual partner (except for Mr. Hand and the International Male underwear catalog). I had hid behind the succulents and jerked off there. I did my earliest experiments with zucchinis in the vegetable garden behind the garage. This is the part of the show that my mom really hates. When she saw it she said, "My god Tim. You did what with my zucchinis? Then I put them in the Tuna Helper." Those squashes' sunlit heat still inside me. The backyard was a minefield of holes in the lawn where I had stuck the rake handle deep in the warm earth to make a tight, hot, wet hole to fuck on dull summer afternoons. There had been a few kisses already, of course. First there was my girlfriend Janet Mauldin in junior high. We kissed on the Journey to Inner Space ride at Disneyland on eighth-grade graduation day.

(Fifties science fiction music and throbbing red lights for Tim's big heterosexual first kiss.)

As I stroked her Marcia Brady hair, we climbed into the royal blue automated car that would carry us into the microscope where we would be shrunk and injected into a water molecule. I kissed her pool-tanned neck as we journeyed through the snowflake field. We put our lips together as those oxygen and hydrogen atoms swirled around us. I stuck my tongue in her mouth as we approached the pulsing red nucleus.

The atom got bigger and bigger, this huge throbbing nucleus hanging in front of us as our wet, wet, wet tongues danced around each other and we got on the ride again and again. Janet and I walked through Tomorrowland with our arms entwined the rest of that June day. I felt the full hot cradling breath of heterosexual privilege wash over me. It floated me up as an offering to the gaping mouth of Walt Disney's hidden queerness, *his* closet the size of Frontierland.

I was thirteen and I had a cute girlfriend. This looks good. She was valedictorian and she would sing a song to me at eighth-grade graduation. The world was fine as I walked arm in arm with Janet Mauldin down Main Street, USA. Everything was good—

(Sound bumps off. Lights get us back to queer reality.)

—except that very soon (once I got the aforementioned pubic hair the next year) I was going to become a giant fruit.

Disneyland would again loom large in senior year of high school as I kissed my first boyfriend Robert at a white-trashy trailer park in Anaheim on New Year's Eve, 1976. The Magic Kingdom's fireworks exploded and Tinkerbell twirled with that frozen frightened-to-death smile on her tightrope descent through the fiery bursts from the Matterhorn while Robert and I stuck our hands in each other's pants a few blocks away. At the last moment, Robert wouldn't put out. We greeted the New Year sulking, drinking cold marijuana tea on opposite sides of a sexless bed.

So, I arrived for my first day at California State University, Fullerton, a reluctant virgin and a proto-punk-rock wanna-be. First class. Eight A.M. Modern Dance 101A. I had been taking dance classes in high school, thus escaping PE and the magnetic pull my head seemed to have for balls of all shapes and sizes. It was part of a pilot program during Governor Jerry Brown's first term called the "Advanced Homosexual Placement and Empowerment Act." Governor Brown came down and gave each of us queer boys a special dance belt embossed with the California state seal. I slipped that dance belt on, then my tights and Patti Smith T-shirt and entered the dance studio. I was about to start my warm-up when my eyes were pulled out of my head by the sight of a sleek dark-haired fellow doing some deep pliés in the corner by the barre. His arm wind-milled over his head. His leg magically circled his ear. The room began to tilt in his direction and I began to slip and slide toward his embrace. Then another cute dancer boy, with an obvious perm and wearing an unfortunate silver unitard, touched him on the arm and said, "Hi, David."

His name was David! That name means "king," I thought. Or, if it doesn't, it fucking well should.

He was totally beautiful. He looked like . . . DAVID BOWIE.

(Bowie music bounces on. The mid-seventies thin white duke period.)

Dancer David, like his namesake, had long articulate legs and fine black-brown hair—maybe a henna highlight rinse. Who knows? David's arms were as long as a giraffe's opera glove, his face set off by a delicate strand of off-white pukka shells around his neck. He, without question, represented one version of the homo physical ideal of 1976, at least as far as my seventeen-going-on-eighteen-year-old eyes could see.

David was the best dancer, and the big queen dance teacher obviously favored him. David dove into each arabesque, devouring the space as he flung himself through the dance combination, scraping the acoustic tile ceiling every time he leapt. I was in the last group and I tried to match his power as I danced only for his eyes.

(Tim struggles as he dances through the combination. Then shrugs. The music stops as Tim stands in a pin spot, only his face illuminated.)

Who was he? Who was this man who would be so much to me? The fuel he would give me still fires lots of kisses. The taste of the food we were gonna eat together is somewhere on the plate at every table where I sit with a man at my side. The touch David taught me is at the tips of my fingers as they dance over the skin of other men. The back of David's neck is suddenly there on another man in a bed fifteen years later, in a strange blue house in Minneapolis. I think I still strive to nuzzle that neck, to sniff my way back to that moment. Of course, I didn't know how he'd change my life and memories then. I just wanted to hold this man with the black-brown hair who looked like David Bowie very close to me.

And who was I at that moment? With the blitzkrieg of puberty, I had come to occupy a world of romantic-cum-homoerotic forces that were a strange cocktail of a nineteenth-century Russian novel and a mid-seventies gay porn movie. A place where Dostoyevsky would get salvation and a locker-room blow job. Maybe I was looking for this imaginary scenario instead of keeping my eyes peeled for the messy real life that just might present itself. I was too smart for my own good and yet not smart enough to know my heart's highways. I finished the dance sequence and caught a glimpse of myself in the thick wire-rim aviator glasses which often made people mistake me for a lesbian separatist from Ann Arbor.

What did I really look like then? Well, my boy-child cuteness had done the usual teenage weedy thing. Hair, bones, and ego had all grown in the most unlikely directions. My cheeks and nose often sported several zits, sometimes in patterns as recognizable as certain constellations (Cassiopeia one week, Ursa Major the next). Nothing that would show up in a dermatological textbook, but enough to cause panic.

I stood near David at one end of the studio and I got incredibly anxious. I began fiddling with my fingers in my new "natural" Afro hairstyle that my barber Big Al Stumpo had given me. My hair had suddenly lost its silky goyish qualities and had become incredibly curly the day after I first jerked off. Big Al Stumpo had tried for years to tame my relentless curls. All during high school, he had forced me to brush through my bristles and comb all those curls to one side. They'd pile up like an electrocuted poodle over my left ear; then, one by one, when no one was looking, those curls would spring back with an audible twang. In 1976, Big Al Stumpo finally gave up. He threw his enormous nicotine-stained hands in the air and said, "Basta! Have it your own way. A curl's gotta do what a curl's gotta do!"

Forcing my fingers to leave my hair, I danced my way a little clumsily through the next part of the teacher's combination, a really hard turn followed by a jump, watching David the whole time, the dance belt under my tights straining to its polyester limits. Somehow, I managed to get through every contraction and release with that dance belt smashing my hard-on against my belly. I wanted time to stop, to walk up to David and begin our pas de deux then and there.

The dance class finally ended. My eyes connected with David's for one wide-screen moment, in the mirror of the rehearsal studio. I saw David walk to his stuff and write something down. He hoisted his dance bag to his shoulder and walked with clipped dignity toward the door. At the last moment, he crisply knelt down by my backpack and slipped a folded piece of orange paper inside. He shot me a nervous look, then quickly left.

I took a breath, counted to three, then raced over to my bag. There it was right next to my Carter/Mondale campaign literature: a flyer for the lesbian and gay student group. I love political organizing! On it he had written, "Call me later. I'll be home around 9:30. David." Then his phone number.

I looked at my watch every three seconds for the next twelve hours. Why do I have to wait so long to call him? I sat in a litter-strewn McDonald's, writing desperate seventeen-year-old's poetry in my journal, having triple-thick shake after triple-thick shake. Finally, at 9:29, my heart playing the bongos, I called David. No answer. I had my sixth chocolate shake. The Big Dipper appeared in pimples on my forehead. I waited a minute and called again. He picked up.

I didn't know what to say. "I got your note," I stammered. "Good."

I could hear a tiny creak in David's voice, too. I listened to his anxious breath flow in and out against my sweaty ear at the receiver.

"Um. Thanks for the note."

"Do you want to come over?" David asked.

"Uh. Okay."

I ran through four red lights on my way to David's sprawling stucco apartment building off Yorba Linda Boulevard, just spitting distance from the little house where Nixon was born (and buried). I walked into his complex, which was called "Vista de los Muchachos del Mar" or something. I walked past the hot tub, overflowing with the usual fraternity-style soapsuds. I sniffed in the tart whoosh of the swooning marigolds in the hot breath of the September Santa Ana breeze: those flowers, sharp chlorine, and Mr. Bubble are what that night in my life smelt like. I climbed up three flights of stairs, found David's unit and knocked softly.

David opened the door slowly, glowing in his fifties red rayon bowling shirt. The smell of herb tea and something baking drifted through from behind him.

"Come in." David opened the door wide.

I had never before visited a friend who lived in his own place. No parents! He showed me around. Even today, I can draw the floor plan as accurately as any architect. The deep shag living room. Piles of books and musical scores. The military organization of the kitchen. The red-lightbulb-lit bedroom with the auto repair shop sign over the bed which read, "All Deliveries Made in the Rear." This was his fucking house; it screamed his independence and his point of view. Someday I will have a place like this for me.

We sat down on the small couch in the living room and we began to talk. I was awed by the extreme adultness of the situation. I kept using big words in absurd sentences.

"You know, David, I think postmodern dance creates an existential situation for self-awareness. And, for me, the artist must be a kind of Nietszchean Übermensch amid stultifying normative bourgeois patterns." I made that up all by myself.

David smiled mysteriously and quickly changed the subject. He told me about his family and growing up. He mentioned he graduated from high school in 1970. I did my simple math and realized he must be at least twenty-four. I was shocked. I had never known anyone quite so old before. Could this relationship work?

David had been much hurt by his twenty-four years of this weird life we've all landed in. He told me about being queer-bashed in front of a gay bar in nearby blue-collar Garden Grove. The attackers stabbed him many times in the neck with an ice pick. He showed me the denim shirt he'd been wearing, still bloody, with the thin tear lines on the fabric where the ice pick skated until the sharp point found its way into his flesh. I still have that shirt. I keep it safe in what's left of my closet.

These last bits of information were a bit *too* adult and scary. I finally shut up.

At last, we got to the main subject. David said, "Tim, I have something very important to tell you. It's something you must know about me if we are to begin an honest friendship. I hope you won't think any less of me. Tim, I'm . . . a musician." In addition to his dance studies at Cal State he was also taking music composition and conducting.

"I have to ask you a question that may really affect how close we can become. What kind of music do you like?" he asked me.

Oh no. A test! Scanning his record collection for a winning answer, I said "I like classical vocal music mostly." I lied, omitting the Patti Smith and the show tunes.

But I had won the daily double! He lit up at this and jumped to his feet. He told me that in his conducting class they were working on the "Amen" from Handel's *Messiah*. He walked to his RadioShack combo record player–eight-track deck, his butt shifting lazily beneath his thrift-shop tuxedo pants with each step. He put a record on the stereo. The phono needle found its scratchy groove and clicked into the ending of Handel's *Messiah*.

> *(The recording of the* Messiah *comes on. The great bit at the end, "Worthy Is the Lamb that Was Slain." Tim speaks in time with the music.)*

David listened and then slowly began to talk about the music as the stately voices vaulted through the cheap speakers.

David said, "Tim, listen, I love this. How simply it begins. The voices make a community. People gathering. Did you ever see *How the Grinch Stole Christmas*? Well, it's like all the Whos down in Whoville or something. Everybody holding hands. Greeting each of the voices. Blessings. Honor. Glory. Power."

David moved slowly nearer and nearer to me on the couch as he spoke. I put down my tea and turned my body toward him, my center of gravity slowly shifting into his orbit.

"Handel does something great here!" he exclaimed. "It's like the tenors start to chat up the baritones. The sopranos start flirting with bull dyke altos. They find a way of understanding this weird world. A way of understanding who *we* are."

David moved his leg up and down against mine as he slowly rocked with the music. I pantomimed a yawn and maneuvered my arm to rest behind his head on the couch. He grabbed my knee, hard, and whispered in my ear.

"And right when it seems it can't get more intense, at that moment all the voices come together and zap it up one more notch. Tim, they remind us to be who we *should* be. Remind us to listen to ourselves. To remember to make the best and truest parts of ourselves grow. To know ourselves. Loving our bodies.

Trusting each other. To nurture those places inside. To give them the light and water and care they need. We know. You and I know who we are. Don't we? We know . . . what we want. What we feel. What we love. This is how we should be!"

David pulled my hand into his. I worried that my palms were too sweaty.

"It's like they're building a doorway for us." He whispered with the music. "The string continuo kicks in and joins the celebration. It's a way out of a place we have been trapped inside of for so long and never knew it. Finally we walk outside together!"

The energy of the chorus built. David put his arms around me and looked into my eyes. His lips moved slowly closer. I felt his breath on my face. Very gently his "Eagle Has Landed" lips touched mine and then—so softly, softly, softly—my new friend David, who looked like Bowie, kissed me!

(A flash-bulb brightness catches Tim in this moment.)

For an instant, I thought my brain would explode. I saw shooting lights and every picture in my photo album race in front of my eyes, a crazily shuffled deck. Then, David broke away and noisily tortured the phono needle across side B of the *Messiah* and said,

(We hear the phono needle abrasively scratch the whole side of the record.)

"I think we've had enough . . . Handel . . . for one evening."

David made a beeline to the kitchen and boiled some water. He shifted us from the yangy "anything could happen" peppermint to soothing "I'm so sleepy" chamomile tea (it's all relative, okay?). Then we held hands some more, listened to the Bach Mass in B Minor, and called it a night.

As I drove down La Habra Boulevard past Richard Nixon's first law office, I felt David's tongue on my lips, his taste as fresh as a bite of an apple that's shiny enough to see your face in.

When I got home, I knew I was going to have to have a hard talk with my mom and dad. I had always subscribed to the slash-and-burn school of relations with parents: fits of outrage, extreme ideological transformations, a knee-jerk willingness to pass judgment on their lives. The usual. I wore my Chairman Mao button on my sleeve to Christmas Eve service. I didn't do these things for me. I did it for them! I needed to provoke my folks and to keep their parental reflexes up. This scorched-earth policy would now cut to the chase. It seemed like a perfectly good time to come out to them.

It was late, really late, when I got back home. My parents were still up. Uh oh. I walked into their bedroom and Bettie and George looked at me, my dad over his *Time* magazine with Walter Mondale on the cover, my mom over her book, a cleavage-festooned romance novel. My mom had her nightly mudpack of Noxzema on her face; the Noxzema had started to harden around the edges and turn a vanilla-wafer-pie-crust brown.

"I think we need to talk," I said. "I know you've been worried about me ever since I first did that summer school musical theater intensive workshop before eighth grade. I wish I could say those worries were unfounded. But I can't. And I just have to tell you something very important. I'm gay."

The pause lasted at least a millennium. My dad rolled his eyes. My mom's book fell to her chin and a bosom on the cover got smeared with Noxzema.

"I just hope you're not going to blame me," she said. "I know they always try to blame the mother."

"I want you to be careful," my dad offered. "Don't wear dresses in public and you won't get beat up."

My mom asked, "Do you have a boyfriend?"

I answered, "Yes, his name is David. He looks like David Bowie. He goes to Cal State Fullerton. I love him. If I'm not home at night, you'll know where I am. I'll bring him over so you can meet him."

"Don't forget to put out the trash," my dad reminded me. "Goodnight, dear!"

They went back to their reading. As I left their bedroom, I, like Miss Peggy Lee, had to wonder: Is that all there is? I slipped out into the kitchen and grabbed the one telephone in our house. I stretched the cord as far as possible from my parents' bedroom. Around the corner. Through the sliding glass door. And called David.

"Hi, David? It's Tim."

"Hi, Hon."

Hon! He called me "Hon." Have any two people ever been more intimate?

We whispered to each other as I twirled the lazy Susan on the kitchen table around and around. I laid the side of my head on the Formica and watched it circle. The salt began to blur with the A-1, which got mixed up with the ketchup. This swirling and twirling of our lives, as lazy as that Susan.

I told him about the Big Conversation with my parents and their lackluster response. David laughed. Then I said, "I need you to meet them sometime soon."

"I want to see you tomorrow," David said. "I want us to make love."

"!"

"I want it to be special. Meet me in the second-floor dance studio at Cal State at 9 P.M. I have the key. I'll be waiting for you."

"I'll see you there, David. Umm, should I bring anything?"

"Well, don't bring any Noxzema, whatever you do!" David said. "Why don't you get a some Vaseline Intensive Care Lotion?"

"Okay. I'll see you tomorrow night."

I heard the soft click as David hung up. I unwound the phone cord, retraced my steps, and very gently placed my telephone receiver back in the cradle as if it were the baby Jesus. I was too excited to go to bed. So I quietly crept out into the backyard . . .

(Time for mood lights! As Tim so often did—see also Some Golden States*—Tim heads for some nookie in the back-yard and slips out of his clothes in the thick, green light.)*

I took off my shirt. Felt the hot wind on my skin. My shoes came next and I felt the dry grass and the snails crackling under my feet. I took off my pants and felt the night creep like David's fingers over my body. I walked across my backyard toward the Valencia orange tree in the redwood-fenced corner.

I had sucked and eaten the sour thrill of a truckload of those oranges. But, now, I pulled one off of the tree and ran it over my face.

(The mysterious orange bobs into view once again. Tim caresses it, then pulls it off the string.)

I imagined David's touch all over my body. Who am I now? Cocksucker. Faggot. Queer. Fruit.

(Naked Tim has peeled the orange and now moves back to the first-row audience folks to place slices in their mouths.)

Fruit is the nicest word we get called. Who wouldn't want to be a fruit? Fruits are delicious, good for you, full of juice. They have a tough skin that can protect them from the shit that the world throws. It covers up their soft and tasty places. You can peel fruit. Expose the prize. Through the layers. To that good place. The fruit of our love, our tears, our sex, our juicy faggotry.

I traced that naked orange down my throat. Over my heart. Felt it wake up my left nipple (two hairs now, FYI), down the hollow of my belly, the pubic hair creeping out like on a Labrador puppy's belly. I bit into that orange and let the juice run down my chest drip, drip, drip off of the end of my dick.

(Tim gets quite messy here what with all the orange juice. Definitely need a shower after this show.)

Dropped it behind my neck (this is where the ice pick was) and it slithered down my back into my ass crack. I pulled its flesh into my mouth and I swallowed a mess of pulpy sloppy orange.

And I felt something hard catch in my throat. It felt as big as a Brazil nut. Tape out. This is an emergency.

(Bright lights. Thunders! Alarums! Excursions!)

I'm choking on the biggest orange seed known to man. I start to gag. I try to cough it up. I fling myself against the fence trying to force it out. I crawl toward my parents' bedroom making strangled gurgle whimpering sounds. WALP MEEEEE!

(Tim goes to audience members and plops his orange-juicy naked butt on someone's lap.)

Please help me. Do the Heimlich maneuver. Don't you read in restaurant restrooms? I guess I'm going to have to (GULP) swallow. Whew. That was close. I'm going to have to be more careful about swallowing. Thanks. Wait. I feel something. Uh oh. It's moving around. This is the thing my Grandma Dutton always warned me about. Don't swallow all those seeds or they're gonna grow inside you! The pissed-off ghosts of a million watermelon seeds are coming back to haunt me. To grow through me. It's getting so big in my stomach. Sprouting. Vining up my spine. My brain is blowing up. Bursting through my body. Sending branches out through my fingertips. Leaves out from behind my ears.

I see flashes of the life to come. No! I don't want to know the future. I'm only seventeen! I just wanna get laid. The visions present themselves.

(Mystical vision music comes on and pulsing, lurid lights.)

If I had gotten that grant this would have been a good moment for a fog machine. Many men in my arms. Much love. Mmmmmm. Much pleasure. This isn't so bad. So we trample each other's vintage sometimes. He did that. You did this. Men that I wrapped myself around hoping they could fix my life. Men that I fled from not knowing how to be what they needed me to be.

Then there is a cloud. There's a terrible plague. This can't be right. Let's change channels. Some of these faggots begin to fall where they fuck. I see that in just five summers this seventeen-year-old will be at Bellevue Hospital visiting an ex-boyfriend, one of the first to become sick. The old round and round stops turning and now we better get wiser.

And there is a vision of a great love. But it's not David. What? I'm going to have more than one lover in my life? As far as I can see they continue to tend each other in their private places even though they don't share a roof or a refrigerator.

Their friends keep dying. Crazy politicians try to hurt us. Control our bodies. Stop our poet's story-shout. "Wait!!! Ghost of Homo Times to Come!!!! Are these the shadows of the things that *will* be, or are they only the shadows of things that *may* be?"

From one of my arm branches, a giant fruit starts to grow. A huge Valencia orange coming right out from my body. It takes on features. A little nose. Cute shaved sides and a green mohawk. How late-seventies CBGB's. Pierced eyebrow.

Oh buff fruit guide, what are you here to tell me?

The fruit pulls itself off the tree and looks at me and and speaks. He sounds just like the pubic hair oracle.

"Silence!"

(The freaky music stops.)

"Ya know. The future is gonna be pretty hard. You're gonna be squeezed to the popping point. You will be hurt by men in ways you can't imagine and oh the hearts and dicks that you will wander across. But each change needs to offer up its fruit. You have to prune the tree to bring forth the fruit. You have to pinch off lots of the buds to let the few grow. You need to bring the new pollen into that blossom to make a new life give fruit. Ya have to sacrifice some to get the other . . . CUT OUT THE DEAD WOOD. . . ."

(We hear faux audience members begin to criticize the show over an audio tape. Tim is pelted with fruit by theater ushers and technical people as he flees naked from taunts.)

*"I can't believe this.
This is the stupidest thing I've ever heard.
I want my money back.
I didn't come here to get depressed.
Enough with the fruit metaphor.
Get a life."*

(Tim shouts.)

STOP!

(The tape bumps off.)

Jeez, haven't you ever seen a dream sequence? I'm sorry. I'm scared. I try to understand what has happened. I hear these voices cause I want them to help me. I get so confused. Don't you? I don't know why I have so many dead ex-boyfriends. I don't understand why I'm such a shit sometimes. I don't know why love hops and hides like Alice's faggot rabbit and tricks us when we least expect it. I want to figure out what I can tell that seventeen-year-old boy before he goes into that dance studio so he won't get so fucking afraid.

Maybe it would help him. Maybe it would help . . . me?

I know that there are these places, okay, maybe they're fruit, inside me that are the treasure of my life.

These seeds of moments where the love rose up toward the sky as my boyfriend Alistair and I walked around and around the Eros statue in Picadilly.

Where the broken heart brought a new life.

Where the poem was as wet as his tongue up my asshole.

(Tim gathers oranges.)

One moment with Ralph Higgs. Some part of me will always be at that Avocado Altar ready to say "I do."

Many many moments with a man named Doug whom I have grown up with and with whom I spent these thirteen ever-changing years that have made me what I am.

One very important moment in my life when I got ready to go be with a man I loved in a dance studio in the California State University system, and that place is still there inside me as close to my skin as that dance belt. But I know that some part of myself keeps whispering in my ear from those places. I hear that whisper as gentle as David's touch. As honest as Doug's heart. As sweet as Alistair's face. As soft as the skin on the inside of Ralph Higgs's arm. The word that I keep trying to hear as it's whispered to my tenderest place inside. So soft, I can just hear it.

"Grow. Grow. Grow."

These places keep calling me, challenging me to reach toward the wet and hot place. And from these places I can make . . .

(Enough of all this! Back to the story.)

But, first things first, I have to shower this orange juice off and get some sleep and buy some Vaseline Intensive Care Lotion and get back to the story. I got a date tomorrow night!

The next day was my eighteenth birthday. I went to Thrifty's and bought an extra-large-size bottle of Vaseline Intensive Care Lotion.

The elderly checkout woman screeched, "Young man, you must have really dry skin!"

"Umm. It's a birthday present—for a new friend," I replied. Then, I vigorously wrote a long time in my journal. I walked up to my special place in the hills of La Habra. I re-read the dog-eared sexy bits from Mary Renault's *The Persian Boy* for the zillionth time. The night fell and it became dark. I bathed and then drove to the California State University at Fullerton. I parked my car by the gymnasium and walked through campus. I breathed in that night's blooming jasmine. Up to that point, my life had felt like it had been written by somebody else. It was hidden in a big weird dusty book on a top shelf, just out of reach. That was about to change. I walked up the stairs into the Performing Arts Building as if I were going up to accept an Academy Award.

I climbed to the second floor and slowly opened the heavy metal door.

The dance studio was dark, except for a single white candle. I tried to see where David was.

A loud scratch as the needle hits the record: "Amen" from Handel's *Messiah* begins to play. I walk into the studio, close my eyes, and fall into the music.

(Tim speaks this over the "Amen" from Handel's Messiah.*)*

David's arms enfold me and we begin to kiss, the kiss I have been waiting my whole life for. Our lips, hungry for each other, make a dance together. David strokes my face gently. This is the touch I have been looking for ever since I learned to tie my shoes—this brother this friend this lover in my arms as the sun rises inside me at last. He bites my neck. Yes. Oh. Fuck. Yes.

David's hands run over my body. Each rolling feeling letting me know myself. My hands run down his back, feeling his chest, his heart beating within. I feel it in the palm of my hand. How much I want this man. I want to climb inside his mouth and swim around inside him, find every hidden wet place. Which I know belongs to me now.

Coming out inside of him. Even as he teaches me the twist and turn of my bones and feelings.

His hair slips through my fingers. He peels my clothes from me. Uncovering a new life underneath. Handel's voices shoot around each other in great waves like all the angels in heaven. I know more than I've ever known anything that this is what God wants me to do. Who I am. What's right for me.

David reaches down and grabs my dick; the touch blows my head to some scattered galaxy I forgot I knew. My eyes look to the back of my brain: stars shoot inside me, through me, his hand moving on me. His lips surround me. Comets whizz by me. A shower of meteors inside my heart.

David and I spin around each other to the music, leaning far back in each other's arms as we twirl. He falls to his knees and puts my cock in his mouth. WOW. All the singing in my head gets really loud. Now. Here. Finally. To find *this* place inside *myself* with another man. I am eighteen fucking years old. I know the touch I want on my skin. Blessing each other with our touch. Blessing our lives as we live them. One big fucking AMEN to guide us through them. The trumpets pull us higher. All the voices reach a peak. You can see everything that you ever hoped you'd be. Everything is right and makes perfect sense in that moment of absolute and perfect rest!

(The music gets real loud. Handel would have loved this bit.)

The music climaxed.
And so did we.

(We hear the music's final, definitive, glorious "Amen!" but the phono needle is stuck at the crucial moment. Slowly fades out skipping. Tim steps into a pool of light.)

Many years later, I stood in front of that dance studio at Cal State, Fullerton, listening to those two young men make love.

I hear the laughter as the phono needle gets stuck at a crucial moment. My fingers touch the chipped corners of that beat-up metal door. I wish I could go in there and join them. But I can't. Can I?

What does that eighteen-year-old boy who I once was have to say to me now? Could he have known the good and terrible places he and David were gonna go together? The short time they would love each other? What really happened to him behind that door? Who the fuck was that teenage boy?

And what do I know, anyway? What do I think I could even tell him? I know I've discovered one or two things about life and love that feel a little bit true. I wish I could whisper them softly in his ear, as he lies on that hardwood floor kissing David, their cum a Milky Way across their chests.

What might that young man tell me, that boy who is now half my life away? Can I hear him? If I really listen, what does he say?

I remembered how eighteen years before, on my eighteenth birthday, I left that dance studio and I wrote in my journal.

I felt David's cum, dry and hard on my belly as I wrote. I sat in my room with the fluorescent green walls and the life-size poster of Oscar Wilde over my bed, a membership premium from PBS, and I wrote these words:

> *(Tape comes on with a voice-over of Tim reading from his journal. Tim performs the fruit dance very slowly and tenderly with the words.)*

> *September 22, 1976*
> *I am eighteen. I love. I don't want this ever to stop. Round and round. The great circle. We die too soon. Lying and hiding chews on us. Must learn to reach out. What else can we do? All wandering in the dark. Nothing to fear. Nothing to lose. I must remember that. Not fearing has brought me the most wonderful man. We will all be dead in a hundred years. All we can do is to touch all the sunlight. All the experience. Eyes meet and a bit of death has been conquered.*

Everyone wants to be touched. We all want it. We often fear it. I am only beginning. Everything is before me now. It's late. The sun is sleeping. I have hardly begun to see. I am eighteen. I am happy. I love David. I love life.

(Tim, our big fruit, slowly reaches up to the sky as the lights fade to black.)

Glory Box

I am currently moving my butt all over the United States (from Salt Lake City to Durham, North Carolina!) doing my solo performance *Glory Box*. The show deals with the situation Alistair, my Australian partner of seven years, and I are facing in a country that gives lesbian and gay couples none of the "special heterosexual rights" afforded all straight married folks. These 1,049 marriage rights, according to the Federal General Accounting Office, include various property rights, health care access, inheritance privileges, and tax benefits. For binational gay couples like us, the BIGGIE of the rights that gay people are uniformly denied is the immigration right that all our straight pals get with their vast buffet spread of heterosexual privilege. Alistair and I face the likelihood that we will soon be forced to leave the United States when his student visa runs out and seek immigration asylum in Canada or the United Kingdom. As you can imagine, this gives a particular urgency to *Glory Box* and my national arts-activism shenanigans!

For almost seven years we have been dealing with the septic tank of homophobic American laws that determine how we can make a life together. This is quite a challenge on top of negotiating the garden-variety difficulties that any two men have trying to relate to each other. In 1997 Alistair's application for a student visa was refused at the American consulate in Australia. Suddenly our lives were thrown into complete chaos. Alistair had to drop out of his MFA program in creative writing. His return plane ticket was no longer valid. We were kept apart for many months at great emotional and monetary expense. It was clear to me that my government had finally declared total war on the most intimate part of my private life as a gay American.

I do have to say that the worst of my experiences as a poster boy during the culture wars doesn't hold a candle to the horrors of trying to live in the United States as a gay citizen in a binational relationship with Alistair. This experience of being threatened with exile has been so much worse than the attacks on my performance work during the NEA 4 controversy ten years ago. Even in the darkest period of George Bush the First, I never thought that I, an American theater artist, not only would have my grants taken away but could eventually be forced to leave my country.

Since I have tried to stay true to my crazy notion that I should always perform about what is most truly on the front burner in my life, I wrote much of *Glory Box* during that period when Alistair and I were separated by the U.S. government. Naturally I am trying to get into the performance—into the *telling*— the steak tartare of feelings that this existential binational relationship is bringing up. Alistair and I have had to fling ourselves around the globe trying to get papers in order so that our love for each other could find a place to grow. You can forget luxuries like wall-to-wall carpeting and a room with a view. We have just wanted to be in the same time zone!

This sometimes overwhelming international dilemma has tapped me back into that faith I had as a tortured gay teenager—

that if I wrote about the hard stuff in my life, it just might make the situation better. Maybe the writing cure could now help me once again to get a lock on a very chaotic situation, the nagging fear that at some point soon Alistair will be forced to leave my country. I have never really lost this trust that the act of writing down my story somehow could alchemically affect how the story might end.

As I travel all over the Unites States and perform *Glory Box*, I am trying to make my case to the nation that this violence and injustice against lesbian and gay couples must stop. The jury is still out. I spend about twenty-five to thirty weeks a year on the road performing and trying to argue this case in theaters and newspapers, on TV and the radio. When I go into a community to do the show, it's an opportunity to be a ruckus-raising agent for change and a lightning rod for the local brew of activists and citizens around issues of gay marriage and immigration.

This is something that solo performance, the ever lean-and-mean culture tool, is especially good at. I assume before I get on the plane that I am parachuting into a community where there is precious little awareness about the gross injustice facing lesbian and gay binational couples. I assume the local press has probably never written about the subject. I assume that the local binational couples (and there are always several, even in tiny communities) are feeling isolated and freaked out by the Kafkaesque injustice of U.S. law that threatens to destroy every one of these thousands of lesbian and gay families.

This is a job for performance art!

What I have discovered is that I can parachute into Cedar Rapids or Austin and point my bright, sweeping klieg light on this injustice. I hit the ground running, ready to raise awareness, anger, and action through the performances. The work starts long before I get off the plane though. I work closely with the Lesbian and Gay Immigration Rights Task Force (LGIRTF), a national organization, to help connect me with local binational gay couples or other folks who have been active on the issue. There are four ways I hope *Glory Box* can energize and activate the communities in which I perform the show: I want to get people involved in the fight against human rights violations against gay people by getting them to join (or start) a local chapter of LGIRTF and raise money; to lobby specific Congresspeople to become sponsors of the Permanent Partners Immigration Reform Bill, which would make U.S. law consistent with almost every other Western country in providing immigration rights for those in committed lesbian and gay relationships; to get virtually every person in the audience to sign a petition in support of the bill, which develops a database of people who have spent a night of their lives thinking about this issue as they watch the performance; and to maximize awareness in the community by having the show serve as a media catalyst for newspaper, TV, and radio stories. I use the crucial tenderized moment at the end of *Glory Box,* which is a very raw and emotional piece, to challenge the audience to do something so that this violence against lesbian and gay lives can stop. It is absolutely crucial for those many hundreds of people in any given city who see the show to get activated around the issue.

The road to performance art hell is paved with good liberal intentions. I am well aware that all my grassroots organizing, performance art agitating, and mass media opining will probably not make the United States join the civilized world any time soon. Most likely Alistair and I ultimately will be forced to leave this troubled country. There is a deeper human goal to all this work, though, beyond the practical, nuts and bolts activism. I am hoping the show can start to do some kinds of emotional and psychic chiropractic adjustments! I am asking the straight folks in the audience to do some heavy lifting and acknowledge their heterosexual privilege and begin to extend their empathy to lesbian and gay relationships. I am also using the show—as well as the urgency of Alistair's and my situation—to ask lesbian and gay people to wake up to the fact that we are second-class citizens in our country. I want the audiences, straight and gay, to begin challenging the millions of signs, signals, and laws our culture delivers that tells us same-sex relationships are worthless. This is a touchy, unjust, ticking bomb that needs to be defused if we are going to secure a more equitable future!

With that futurity hovering just beyond our grasp, I also need to admit that we are clearly going to have to engage beyond the stage in order to defuse that bomb. In addition to the script of *Glory Box*, I need to give you an example of a different kind of performance I did recently. It's not a performance whose text is in this book. In fact, it wasn't scripted and it's very much an in-progress kind of thing. It's a performance that any of us can do on a social stage at courthouses, city halls, or county clerks' offices. It doesn't take any rehearsal. On Valentine's Day 2001 Alistair and I tried to get a marriage license. There are those who might think that celebrating Valentine's Day by being refused a marriage license is not the most romantic way to mark the holiday. I suppose I can understand that sentiment, but personally I can't imagine a more real, emotional, and tender way to escape from the Hallmark card platitudes of February 14. I wanted to mark Valentine's Day with my partner of seven years by protesting how gay folks' relationships are treated so disrespectfully in our country. I hope some day Alistair and I won't need to spend our V-Day putting ourselves in the position where our relationship is refused validation by a governmental official behind bulletproof glass, but that's life in America in the twenty-first century!

Since more straight folks choose to get engaged or married on Valentine's Day than on any other day of the year, Marriage Equality California staged rallies all over the state to advocate for equal civil marriage rights for gay couples. Gathering outside the aforementioned courthouses, we wanted to draw attention to the injustice lesbian and gay partners face in our country by being denied those pesky 1,049 special heterosexual privileges of marriage.

Alistair and I went to the February 14 demonstration at the marriage license office at the Beverly Hills Courthouse. As gay couples and supporters huddled for support in the shadow of governmental buildings that do not respect our humanity, rally speakers spoke passionately against the injustice of not allowing gay and lesbian couples the right to marry. Then—the big moment—the couples who were planning to request a marriage license prepared to challenge the laws of the state.

Alistair and I joined many couples who were going to attempt to apply for a marriage license. First things first, we filled out the form. Immediately the sexism and homophobia of the document leapt out at us and we quickly crossed out the word "bride" and "corrected" the form so there were two grooms! We took turns writing down in our blocky letters our fathers' names and what our mothers were called before they were married. This was so moving—this ritual of calling up the parents, putting our names and our love on the line.

Sticking close to the nice lesbian couple in front of us—I always look to dykes for moral support—we went through the metal detectors, approached the glassed-in processing windows, and gave our form to the official. It was refused, of course. She read from a form (they were prepared) and told us that in the state of California a marriage can only be between a man and a woman (who knew?!?!). The woman behind the glass, who was very sweet and seemed a little ashamed of her job this particular day, advised us to take it up with our elected officials. Always ready to climb on my soapbox, I said to her, "I know this is not your fault, but I want you to know that because we don't have the same rights as straight Californians, my partner and I will be forced to leave the country next year." She shrugged and tried to melt under the counter. We walked out the double doors clutching our rejected marriage license application.

I have never felt a more tangible denial of my equality than when I was told I couldn't get a license while straight couples breezed by around me. It was almost a ritual *performance* of how I am denied the human rights of relationship in my country, a sur-real *rehearsal* of second-class citizen status. How clear things became having a bureaucrat explain to me that my relationship of seven years was worth nothing, while to my right a straight cou-ple who seemed to have just met at a singles bar in Marina Del Rey got the seal of approval.

Well, that's how we spent our Valentine's Day. By the time we got home later that afternoon, we were too beat to go have the romantic dinner in West Hollywood. To stand there in front of the courthouse filling out the marriage license form with my husband Alistair had been very powerful for me but I was definitely ready for an early night. As we drove home down Venice Boulevard, a vision started to take form in my mind's eye. I could see a time when filling out this marriage license form wouldn't just be a para-theatrical activist gesture, doomed to rejection. There was a sweet-ness to imagine that some day in the future we might actually live in a country where gay people's love would also be valued. I will leave you now as Alistair and I are driving home. Conjuring that future hovering beyond our grasp is going to require many such hopeful and quixotic acts from all of us, a thousand such fierce ges-tures—a thousand such *performances*—that dare to tell the truth that our love is worthy and our hearts are strong.

I have a big story to shout right now on stage doing *Glory Box* or in front of courthouses. It fills my memory. It's a story of how I met a man from another land and how I want to be with him, but America doesn't allow such things. I need to tell this story or I will go crazy. When I tell this story I can howl out the rage I feel both at our backward government and at my own shortcomings as a man and a lover. I can draw the attention to this stark injustice. Telling this story becomes a completely nec-essary act of saying what has happened as a means of negotiating, even securing, a more empowered relationship with an uncertain future.

My journeys with *Glory Box* have been a real confirmation to me of the potential power of performance and theater to really get a loud alarm bell ringing. As I travel the country and abroad doing the show, I have been reassured that what we do at these performance spaces and theaters can have a huge impact, a clear ripple effect, on both our inner selves and on our social identities.

(The set is a backdrop with a huge collage of maps from all over the world. Most of these maps come from Tim's child-hood subscription to National Geographic. *To the right is a big, old hope chest, aglow in light. Tim enters and runs all around the stage. The followspot ballyhoos—Tim is pleased to have just learned this term during a technical rehearsal in the Midwest. It means the spot waves all around like Las Vegas or something—finally the spot hits Tim.)*

Okay, Okay. I got to show you something.

I want to show you something very important. If I wait one more second my brain will explode all over you nice people in the front row and make a big mess. I want to show you my box.

I want to show you my glory box.

My partner Alistair is from Australia—this will loom large in the show. Alistair told me that in Australia what we here in the States call a HOPE CHEST, the thing that teenage girls put shit in to prepare themselves for the eventual servitude of marriage, in Australia, they call a GLORY BOX. Now, clearly, I am not a teenage girl (though I do share with that demographic an unwholesome obsession with *Dawson's Creek!*), nonetheless I have decided that I need a glory box too. I'm going to keep in it all kinds of good things my culture gave me as a young gay boy to prepare me for my queer life ahead—the gay-positive role mod-

els, the encouragement of gay relationships, the after-school programs . . . HMMM. Well, since I actually didn't get any of those
positive things, instead I'll put in the glory box the things I did
get. I'm going to put in that glory box the hundreds of times I
was called a sissy or faggot as a kid growing up on the streets of
this country. I'm going to put in that glory box the thousands of
signals I received from my culture that told me my relationships
with other men aren't worth shit and would never be acknowledged. I'm going to put in that glory box the zillion feelings
related to the fact that since my relationship with Alistair is not
acknowledged by my fucked-up country we may be forced to leave
our home in the United States to go to a civilized country that
does value gay people's love, like Great Britain, South Africa, Australia, Germany, or Canada.

Oops, I'm getting ahead of myself. I have found, over many
years of performing, that you should never put the overbearing
political rant in the first forty-five seconds of the show. It's much
better to wait for at least one good joke and perhaps some cheerful nudity!

(Tim lounges odalisque-like on the hope chest.)

I recently moved my mom's hope chest into my house. It is
a big old cedar thing, heavy as a bank safe, smell as pungent as the
day it was bought. When I was a kid, I was endlessly fascinated
with this hope chest. Even the words themselves were a mystery.
HOPE CHEST. I took these words literally. I was sure that they
referred to an actual part of the body. If I looked in an anatomi-
cal reference book, I would see that HOPE CHEST was behind
the sternum and to the left of the heart. We all know it's there. I
imagined that this was the place inside us, a place where we could
put the things we hoped for.

I floated this notion out to my mom one afternoon after
kindergarten as she was doing the ironing while watching *Art
Linkletter's House Party* on TV. "Mom?" My voice is small,

unformed, a tender flower on the side of a deserted road. Go with me on this, okay?

"Yes, dear."

"Is a hope chest a place inside me? A place where I put things I hope for?"

My mom was preoccupied with her ironing and didn't want to entertain the queries of her young queer son, but she did her best. She said, "Why, no, dear. A hope chest is something that was given to me when I was a girl. It's there at the end of your dad's and my bed. It was a special chest for me to put the things that I would need when I was married."

This was not the answer I had hoped for. This seemed to say that the hope chest was for practical things, like dishes and linens. "What kind of things?"

"Oh, you know, practical things, like dishes and linens. That glass bowl there on the table was in the chest for years before your dad and I were married."

This was sounding worse by the minute. I gave her one last chance.

"Didn't you ever put things you hoped for in there?"

"Hmm. Well . . . yes . . . I always hoped that I would have a good little boy like you, and here you are." I didn't buy her mom-shtick one bit. "Maybe the little girl that you will one day marry already has a hope chest and she's putting things in it to prepare for your marriage! Isn't that a lovely thought?"

"Eeew. I hate girls! I'll never get married."

"You do not hate girls and you will too get married. Now, darling, mother's busy. Why don't you go and have a graham cracker?"

Clearly, I wasn't going to get a straight answer from my mom. So I went into my parents' bedroom, heavily curtained against the hot Southern California sun. I sat on my mom's hope chest at the foot of the bed, my little legs only reaching halfway down to the floor as they knocked against the cool front. The wood was cool against my legs. The weight of my body made my thighs squish out flat against the wood, making my upper leg look big, fatty piggy big leg (I had a bit of a complex about my thighs when I was five). It looked like a frog's leg. Or a girl's! Which my brother told me was worse. I tensed the small muscles in my legs to make them look more butch. They bounced up and down against the cedar, preparing me for a future life of going to the gym and performing repetitive physical action as a means of covering up negative feelings about my body. That gets old, though, doesn't it?

So I slipped down to the mashed, no-longer-deep-polyester-shag carpet and I opened the lid of the chest. I had looked in the hope chest many times before. This was one of my favorite rituals, almost as good as turning on the gas jet in the fireplace and waiting a good twenty seconds before throwing a match in and feeling the volcano blast of the natural gas singe the hairs on my arms and eyebrows.

I breathed the universe of the hope chest into my small nose. The tart smell of the cedar wood was delicious, dangerous, narcotic. I knew everything that was in there already; I'd cataloged it as carefully as if I were the youngest employee of the Smithsonian. The smart fake-chinchilla bolero jacket my mom had bought for her trip to Mexico City in 1957, the red leather high heels from that same vacation, the carefully wrapped-up front pages of the *Los Angeles Times* from the few days after Kennedy was shot, just the year before. On the front page the day after JFK's funeral there's John-John, who is almost exactly my age, saluting crisply. He's wearing a sort of sailor-influenced ensemble, which was an outfit that I coveted until I was nine years old.

Peeking to make sure my mom was not headed this way . . .

(Tim stands in the hope chest, takes off his clothes.)

. . . I took off my clothes, my Beany and Cecil T-shirt and Hawaii-inspired mom-sewn baggy jam surfer shorts that she had made

from a ninety-nine-cent pattern from JCPenney. I carefully slipped one foot into the chest and the other soon followed.

(Tim sits in the box, hoping that the theater got one without splinters and big enough to fit his naked butt into!)

I rubbed that chinchilla over my body, trying to wake up my hope chest. In case you're wondering, at the age of five my body was much smaller and I had no pubic hair. Then I lay down in the box, wrapped in chinchilla, and closed the lid of the hope chest over me. Now I knew five-year-olds like me were not supposed to climb inside boxes and close the lids. I had heard the horror story about the twins down the block who had gotten trapped in an old refrigerator and suffocated. Climbing into a hope chest and closing the lid on top of you seemed much different. This wasn't a terrible thing you would read about in *Reader's Digest* Drama in Real Life, this was more like something my favorite breakfast cereal character, Count Chocula, would do on a rainy afternoon while his mom was ironing his vampire capes.

My mom walked into the bedroom to hang up my father's shirts. I knew this would be an ideal moment to frighten her, one of my main pleasures at the age of five. I could jump out with a flourish and a scary growl, her naked five-year-old son wrapped in chinchilla fur, and make her toss the shirts in a fright.

"Beware the wrath of COUNT CHOCULA!"

But I didn't. I silently crossed my arms over my chest, my own hope chest inside me. I felt safe in there. I felt full of hope.

(A pause. Tim uncrosses his arms, eyes the audience, gets out of the hope chest and back into his clothes.)

Alistair and I were moving my mom's hope chest recently into the house where we live in Venice Beach. Alistair was helping me load it into the hatchback of my tiny, jade-green Geo Metro.

My back straining against the weight of my mom's chest, so to speak, I said, "Damn, this thing weighs a ton! Did your mom have a hope chest?"

Alistair, who is of a thoughtful nature, walked away from the car, leaving me holding the weight of my mother's chest and pondered. "Hmmm. No, she didn't have a hope chest, but she did have a glory box. I think that's the same thing." Then he tossed me the rope.

"A what?!?" I started to tie the chest down.

"A glory box."

"You've got to be kidding, right?"

"What?"

"You really call them GLORY BOXES?"

"Well, of course. What's so strange about that?"

"It just sounds so nasty. So below the belt. It makes me want to fuck your glory box."

Alistair looked around to see if anyone had heard. "Don't be vulgar!" Alistair snapped the rope on my fingers.

Now that's more like it! Glory box! This changes everything. A glory box transforms a bland Southern California maiden into a resplendent Australian Joan of Arc astride her glory box! I've decided that I need a glory box right now in my life—because Alistair and I are going through a hard time trying to stay together in a country that doesn't want us—and I'm going to gather the things I need and put them into my glory box and make our future happen!

(Bright headlights slash the space, pinning Tim against the map backdrop. We're in the operating-room starkness of a customs-immigration checkpoint.)

In the future. I am now in the future, okay? Got it, smart audience? Here in the future I'm waiting outside of Immigration and Passport Control at Los Angeles International Airport. I'm waiting for Alistair to get through U.S. Customs.

"What if they don't let Alistair into the country?"

I'm being mugged by this thought.

"What if they don't let Alistair into the country?"

I have quickly breezed through the U.S. citizens' gate after getting off the plane from Sydney and I'm waiting now for Alistair to get through the slow-moving foreign nationals line. I spot his lanky handsome self and give a wave.

The two swoops of light brown hair that fringe either side of his forehead are a curtain, a theatrical gesture always halfway in the process of going up on the second act. Alistair has moved through his life with the graceful surprise of a tender young man who couldn't completely believe that he had actually managed to escape from his family, twelve years of Roman Catholic boys' school, and remote Western Australia to make a life with me in California.

His sweet vulnerability has opened up a place in me that I thought I had put in cold storage long ago. This young man has taken a big chance in his life and let his love for me pull him from one end of the world to the other.

The faith and tenderness I have seen in his face each time he has looked up at me from a sleepy morning pillow in London or New York or Sydney almost overwhelms me.

How can this man trust me so? How can he be so crazy to link his life with mine? Doesn't he know what damaged goods I am? Someone should tell him! Doesn't he know how fucked-up I am? Doesn't he know how scarred I am by what happened to me when I was nine years old?

(Following a gesture of Tim's arm, a stab of diagonal warm light bisects the stage.)

It was a day of judgmental Twinkies being smashed in my face. I was nine years old. I was walking down Russell Street with my friend Scott—he was a second cousin of President Richard Nixon and we lived in Whittier, the president's hometown. So you can see, Republicans have been fucking with me for as long as I can remember. We walked, free-associating as young boys will do. We walked by a house that was widely regarded as the most tasteful in our neighborhood, much respected for its impressive series of ceramic elves decorating the winding walkway to the front door!

Scott said to me, "When I grow up, I'm going to marry that cute girl in our class Gail Gardener and we're gonna live in that house with the ceramic elves." Then Scott looked at me as if he thought he deserved a ninety-nine and a happy face on a spelling test.

This was a new subject and I sensed that it meant trouble. I bought some time and walked silently along, my *Lost in Space* lunch box clanking against my leg. My *Lost in Space* lunch box filled with my favorite lunch. A sandwich, made with Wonder Bread of course, and layers of delicious Jif smooth peanut butter and Welch's grape jelly with a generous crunchy handful of Fritos corn chips in between. (MMM, all that delicious sugar, oil, and salt! Everything a young American needs to grow strong.) Next to my Will Robinson, played by the adorable tow-headed Billy Mumy, thermos was a special treat: a Twinkie in its crisp, confident plastic wrapper.

I knew I was making a mistake before I even opened my mouth. "But, Scott, when I grow up, I want to marry you and live in the house with the ceramic elves!" He looked at me as if I had suggested that we tap dance together to the moon.

"What! Boys can't get married to each other. Everybody knows that."

"Why not?"

"They just can't."

"Why?"

"Because."

"Because why?"

Clearly, logic wasn't working so Scott pushed me hard with both hands, knocking me into the deep dusty ivy of my Congregationalist minister's front yard. We all knew rats lurked and prospered in the dark gnarly labyrinth of the ancient ivy. I drowned in the dirty green.

Scott jumped on me, looking around to see if anyone had heard me ask him to marry him. "Take it back! Say you don't want to marry me and live in the house with the elves!"

"I won't take it back!"

"Take it back, or I'll give you an Indian burn." He pinched my side hard and then grabbed my wrist with both hands and twisted in opposite directions. I screamed.

"Do you take it back?"

"I won't take it back!"

He Indian-burned my other wrist. I probably could have fought him off, but part of me had longed for some kind of closeness with Scott ever since kindergarten. Being tortured by him would have to do. You've all been there. My lunch box had fallen open near my head, revealing the Twinkie in all its cellophane splendor. Scott got a horrible idea and grabbed the Twinkie in his little fist.

"Take it back or I'm going to jam this Twinkie in your throat and kill you!"

"I won't take it back!" The strength of my high-pitched voice surprised me. "When I grow up, I'm going to marry you and live in the house with the ceramic elves!"

A look of shock and frustration passed like bad weather across Scott's face. Scott shoved the Twinkie into my mouth and held his small dirty palm over my lips. I exploded with cellophane and Twinkie goo. Now, I knew that even more than climbing into boxes with lids, kids weren't supposed to suck on cellophane. I took the warnings on the dry-cleaning bags seriously. I knew I'd reached my Twinkie limit and I would have to take it back. Fortunately, my oldest brother had just taught me the week before a special trick. Whenever anyone is tormenting you and wanting you to be untrue to yourself and take something back, all you have to do is cross your fingers and put them behind your back. This erases it. In case you thought this stopped working in childhood, it didn't. It still works in adult life, especially around relationship issues! I quickly crossed my fingers behind my back.

"Alright! I take it back." Scott got off of me. He looked so strange. He kicked me, grabbed his math book and banal *Bonanza* lunch box, and stormed off to school and the rest of his life filled with petty disappointments and three wives who would fear him. (Don't ask me how, I just know!)

I lay there on my back, pinned to the earth. Surrounded by primordial ivy dust and Twinkie. I pulled my crossed fingers from underneath my back and held them up to the sky. The crossing of those fingers negated my "I take it back," my one triumph over his small tyranny. I held them up to the hot California sun, and as I repeated the words they gathered steam inside me. "I will never take it back. I will never take it back. I will never take it . . ."

(Tim crosses back to the customs-immigration area.)

. . . back at Customs, Alistair is just a few people back in the line behind what promised, hopefully, to be a friendly female Customs and Immigration officer. (We thought we might have better luck with a woman officer. You gotta have a system!) Since meeting in London in 1994, Alistair and I have flung ourselves all over the world to try to find a way to make a life together. In spite of a Sears catalog of differences between us—nationality, age, accent, music (his Trip Hop CDs versus my Broadway musical soundtracks, that almost did us in!)—we consistently found ourselves pulled closer and closer on the ever shaky earth. That meeting in London was followed by a rendezvous in Glasgow, Scotland (city of Alistair's father's birth), an assignation in New York, and finally a home together in LA. This particular journey to Sydney had been purely to extend his student visa so that we could gain a little breathing time. So this little piece of paper that will give us six months more of our life together is costing us about twelve thousand dollars. I'm sending the bill to the White House!

Alistair and I have been flying through a day and a night and a day from Sydney. At this point we both have bags under our eyes bigger than our carry-on luggage crammed under the seat in front of us.

As soon as we got on the plane, Alistair and I had done what we could to make ourselves COZY! The pursuit and attainment of coziness is a crucial ideological underpinning of our relationship. As we walked onto the 747 we each grabbed eight blankets and eleven pillows—more than our share, but we suffer in so many other ways! Then we pulled up the armrest, upholstered our seats with the pillows, put a blanket over our laps, "cozied" and cuddled close, kissed a little, and acted like we were normal people! What nerve! I don't know if you've noticed that when two dykes or two fags act like normal people and show their affection in public, that intimacy sort of crackles through the cabin. It's almost as if the captain had made a special announcement over the PA system of the airplane.

"Attention. This is Captain Straight Whiteman. Welcome to Flight 222, nonstop service from Sydney to Los Angeles. Would everyone please gawk at the Australian and American flaunting their disgusting love in row 41?"

The entire men's soccer team from Knoxville, Tennessee, wheels around and stares. In spite of the stares of the Men of Tennessee, it does feel like international air travel is one of the few homophobia-demilitarized zones available to us. There are those federal laws against making nasty jokes plus everyone is scared the plane might fall out of the sky so it keeps them on good behavior.

The 747 whooshed endlessly over Micronesia while they showed the seventh of eleven movies on the flight, the one I was most looking forward to, *Free Willy 2*. I had my headset on as I waited for that thrilling phallic moment when the whale jumps over the wall. It's a liberation narrative, let's face it. I looked over and saw that Alistair wasn't watching *Free Willy 2* and in fact he was looking a little green about the gills.

"How ya doin'?" I asked him.

"I'm okay. I'm just pretty scared of how this immigration stuff is all going to go off."

The large pink tuxedoed killer whale had finally made his presence felt.

"What'll we do if something goes wrong and they don't let me in?" Alistair says. "Our whole life is in LA. I can't just go back to Australia. What if they don't let me in like in ninety-seven when they wouldn't give me my visa and we were apart for so long while I was stuck in Australia?"

Now, I have to admit that I wanted to get back to *Free Willy 2*. But let's be fair to me for a moment, shall we? Alistair and I had been processing this anxiety for weeks! I'm not proud of it, but I said a little dismissively, "We'll-Be-Fine!" with that annoying American Optimism that makes Americans seem like pampered, retarded children to the rest of the fucked-over world. I repeated the words, kissing Alistair in time with each word. "We'll-Be-Fine!" But now I'm on a roll. "Fuck *Free Willy 2*! It's so unfair. We're not doing anything wrong. This double standard totally sucks. . . ."

(As Tim winds up into a big rant, the stage turns deep, capillary-busting red.)

"Just because we're two gay men, we can't do what all our straight friends can do—get married and get a green card. The INS just rolls out the red carpet for the fabulous heterosexuals exercising their goddamned privilege. I am so pissed that the fucking U.S. government does not recognize our relationship. Do you know, Alistair, I was on the Internet last night, on the Lambda Legal Freedom to Marry Web site. Do you know there are 1,049 rights, 'special heterosexual rights' that our straight friends get the instant they get married that you and I will never have even if we are together the rest of our lives? I get so mad! I believe right now that for heterosexual people to get married while gay people can't is a completely immoral act. As immoral an act as going to a restaurant that doesn't serve black people, joining a country club that won't allow Jews. I feel so oppressed by THE TYRANNY of heterosexual hegemony and the complete denial of my civil right of marriage! ARARRGHH!"

In case you were wondering, this was the overbearing political speech I had referred to at the top of the show . . .

(Whew! Lights restore back to normal.)

. . . and Alistair had heard my stump speech too many times before. "Tim, it's just me here. Let's not start. I need to get some sleep. Okay?"

"Okay." I indulged a quick sulk at my rant being interrupted, only a 3.4 on the Sulk-O-Meter. Then I tried another approach. I slipped a hand under the blanket that covered Alistair's lap and began to creep my way finger by finger below that more thrilling equator of the waistband of his baggy Dolce & Gabbana pants.

I felt the rise and fall of my lover's belly, the skin warm and reassuringly full of breath as I let my palm rest there. The stomach could be such a battlefield for men: SUCK IT! BUST IT! CUT IT! CRUNCH IT! Alistair and I had recently begun a campaign to claim the flesh in each other's perfectly reasonable stomachs as a new site of sexiness. It just seemed ridiculous that after years of sleeping together, spooning in bed, we would touch each other's bellies and we were still sucking them in! Let's vow never to do that again! Come on! "Belly Liberation Now! You have nothing to lose but your Ab-Busters!" (This is a digression, I know, friends tell me I should cut it, but I think it's important!)

Circling a caress around his navel, I made a Munchkin-Land yellow brick road spiral outward, heading further south. I dove down all the way to the South Pole and carefully cradled Alistair's soft cock in my hand. I think the soft penis is highly underrated. That moment of vulnerability in the penis touches me somewhere quiet, reminds me how fragile and susceptible men's bodies really are. There's something so cheerful, so accessible, so avuncular about a man's soft dick. Now I know there are certain academic discourses about the cock as sword, phallus as weapon, etc. But that kind of rhetoric crashes against the sweet reality of the recumbent, melancholic, almost Chekhovian, soft dick. You can quote me on that. A soft penis is much more like a panicked Clark Kent searching madly for a phone booth to do his makeover. I gently stroked and coaxed Alistair's soft dick to see if this was indeed a job for Superman. Alistair raised one brow and shifted his hips out of my orbit. Once again I was not going to become a member of the Mile High Club; for this trip was not for pleasure.

I had another sulk, a 7.8. To console myself, I went back to muttering about the tyranny of heterosexist hegemony and the complete denial of my civil right of marriage. This made me feel better.

Ya know, I talk a lot about this marriage stuff these days. I'm going to keep talking about it as long as lesbian and gay folks' relationships are under attack in America, but the truth is the one time a man asked me to marry him, all I could say was no.

(Tim moves close to the audience to confess and conspire.)

It was my ex-boyfriend John in 1982. We had broken up the year before when I was twenty-two. A few months after we had broken up John began to have some health problems: skin trouble, night sweats, blood not clotting, all the scary symptoms of what very soon we would immediately recognize as the early signs of AIDS. Almost a year after we had split, John slipped a letter under the door of my crummy apartment on Avenue B and Fourth Street in New York and asked me to marry him. It might seem strange to you that he would ask someone he had broken up with months before to marry him, but John needed to get a clear answer of whether I would ever be his man.

I said no. I wasn't ready to hitch my Manhattan ego-grubbing star to anybody at that time in my life. John had his answer and knew he should give up on me. But some part of me also gave up on myself. At the age of twenty-three I was terrified that I would never be able to commit my love to another man. Sure, the next year I met my boyfriend Doug and we would be together for thirteen years. We would be as much one another's husbands as I could ever imagine being, but we never actually wed. I don't know why. I know it's too late now. Just like it was too late for John and me. John, who has been dead these many years. So I am left with this one proposal in my life—a young man on the Lower East Side asked me to wed and all I could say was NO. Why would it be so hard for me to say those words I DO? Almost as hard as I LOVE YOU.

I mean, I feel practically married to my partner Alistair. For seven years we have loved and tamed each other well, but we struggled in the early years of our relationship to be able to say the words I LOVE YOU to each other. It was very hard for us. Well, that's not quite true. Actually, *I* had struggled for years to say "I love you." I am not an easy date. If you take one message away from the show take this one—WASPS TAKE WORK!

Why was it so hard for this WASP to wrap my lips around those three little Anglo-Saxon words? Maybe because it's much easier to just wrap my lips around Alistair's juicy Aussie dick? I don't know if you've noticed, but when you say "I love you" when your mouth is full of hot Aussie cock, the words just come out all garbled. You might as well be asking for a cheeseburger. Plus, I don't think you should say the words I LOVE YOU unless you're sure that you will mean them for a minimum of thirty-six to forty-eight months. They need to have a longer shelf life than a quart of milk! And what if you say them to someone and they don't say them back? That's happened to me. It's horrible! I don't want to toss the jewels to someone unless I'm pretty sure I'm gonna get them back, maybe with a little compound interest! For this reason, I kept those words locked away for the first two years of our relationship and didn't say them to Alistair, even though I did love him, and even though he had come from the other side of the world to be with me.

There came a point when this state of affairs was ridiculous, even for a fucked-up person like me. I had to acknowledge that I had a disability. I had the speech impediment peculiar to the male of our species—this tremendous difficulty in translating powerful feelings within into tangible spoken language. I would do whatever it took to work through this and learn how to say "I love you." I'm a systems kind of guy, so I thought I could use my theater voice exercises to teach myself how to say "I love you." I LOVE YOU! I began practicing saying the words I LOVE YOU to my favorite photograph of Alistair. It's the one from Halloween 1995 and Alistair is wearing my dad's sailor suit from World War II (don't ask!). I looked at Alistair long and lean in the Navy uniform my dad had worn in the South Pacific and I said, "I love you!" Like an actor practicing his lines.

I knew I had to ease into saying the words real-time. I'd whisper the words when Alistair was nearby, but when he couldn't actually hear me. He would be washing dishes or listening to music on his Walkman and I would nonchalantly come by to put away some towels and I would whisper out of the corner of my mouth, "I love you."

Alistair began to worry that I was going mad with all this mysterious mumbling. He confronted me and I was forced to let him in on what I was doing. He thought it was a little weird, but it was okay if I needed to practice as long as he knew when the sessions were.

This began the most fruitful period of I LOVE YOU practice. We would begin designating I LOVE YOU rehearsal sessions. Now I wish I could say that I'm making up this part of the show to make it a better story or something ... BUT I'M NOT! Alistair and I would be lying in bed reading (Alistair is the only person I know who actually reads Foucault for before-bed pleasure reading), and I would lean over and ask if we could practice now. He would set his book, *Discipline and Punish,* down and I would whisper in his ear, "I Love You." You know what, over time I became less afraid of the tartness, of the bite of those scary words. Maybe this old dog can still learn some new tricks. If I can say "I love you" maybe I can also find the way my lips can say some other things, like "Will you marry me?" or "I do." Not that we really want to support a corrupt, irredeemable, bourgeois institution or that I would be allowed to marry Alistair even if I could say the words! But, unless I can say them, I'll never know, will I?

Will ... You ... MMMMMM ... MMMMMM ... MMMMM

(That delicious "MMM" pulls Tim back to the center stage
Customs and Immigration area.)

MMMeanwhile, back in Customs in the future, I am waiting for Alistair, who is stuck in a line that hasn't moved in a week. I decide to use the time productively by having an anxiety attack. "OH, GOD, WHERE'S MY PASSPORT? I'VE LOST IT! I'M DOOMED!!!" I don't even know why I'm worrying, I've already made it through Customs and don't even need my passport. There it is, right where I left it in my back pocket. But how can I be sure it's my passport? Maybe someone has switched it on me? I pull out my passport to make one hundred percent sure that it's mine. I open the document up and look at the picture. It's me. WHEW. It's a good photo. Winsome smile. Good hair day. I'd gone to some lengths to get this good photo, the five separate photo shoots. The trip to West Hollywood to the b/w studio with the flattering "Golden Era of MGM musicals" backlighting. Anyone would say this is a good passport photo, but if this is such a good passport photo why do my brown eyes look so sad? I look into my eyes and I see a hurt there, a trail of clumsy love and dead friends stretching far behind me. I know if I had a visa stuck in my passport for every time I had said no to love or shoved overboard some feeling that scared the shit out of me, if all those visas were in my passport it would be as thick as the Manhattan phone book.

I close the passport and stroke the smooth plastic of the cover with the American eagle on the cover. What an unhappy creature that eagle is! If you have a passport, when you get home tonight take it out and look at it. This eagle looks right out of the Third Reich with its butch "oh, this is my good side" profile, clutching those razor-sharp Ninja arrows, one to pierce the heart of each of our deepest aspirations. And in the other talon is a limp olive branch. I know, I paid attention in civics class, but this is clearly just an afterthought that some spin doctor threw in to soften the image. This is a VERY unhappy bird! I look at my U.S. passport in my hand and at Alistair waiting in line and I think to myself, "Wait, this is crazy. Why can't I just toss my passport to Alistair there in line? Share it with him. Just like I share my life and my bed with him. Why can't I share my nation with him? Invite him to share my citizenship with me?" Never forget, this is what every straight person can do and no gay person can—get married, get a green card, and share their country with someone they love. If we could do this we'd already be home. Alistair would already have a green card or have become a citizen long ago. We would have gone through the quick line, gone home, dropped off our bags, gone to the beach, had a Jody Maroni Sausage Kingdom chicken chorizo sandwich, gone home, and had quick sex before sleeping off the jet lag for sixteen hours!

But since I can't share my country, share my citizenship with my love, I see my partner of many years looking scared to death stuck in a U.S. Customs line with his Australian passport clutched over his heart. His Australian passport with a kangaroo and an emu on the cover. Let's compare these two passports, shall we? These are HAPPY animals, CHEERFUL animals! That emu and the kangaroo seem like they are planning a BBQ down under. They're preparing the tasty Vegemite canapés. They'll give every-one one of those fifty-gallon-drum cans of Foster's lager. They want all their guests to get laid, but our cranky American eagle just doesn't want anyone to have a good time.

Was it only two nights before that we were still in Australia, laying together in an airless hotel room in Sydney, hot as hell, summer in February down under, in King's Cross Hotel? We had had pre-international-travel comfort sex and had both just come. Our bodies were still dewed with sweat, making our skin stick together with a tiny wet sound. Forcing myself to wait the required ninety seconds post-orgasm that I know a sensitive guy like me needs to wait before a new non-intimacy related activity can be introduced, eighty-seven, eighty-eight, eighty-nine . . . (I can hold out the whole time. I took a workshop.) . . . ninety! I let my arm dangle off the edge of the bed, retrieving my map of the world from the floor, then spread it out before us like a vast, laminated, open-all-night midtown Manhattan delicatessen menu.

"God, the world is a big fuckin' place," I whispered with a whistle as my eyes darted over the colorful map from the Bering Strait to the Himalayas. I covered my eyes, pretending that I was preparing myself for Double Jeopardy, "World Geography for a Thousand." "The capital of the Sudan . . . What is Khartoum? The capital of Slovakia . . . What is Bratislava? What if you could live any-where, where would it be? Belgium? A little boring, but they have that cute pissing boy everywhere. Ecuador? My brother lived on a volcano there for a year doing his Ph.D. Kathmandu? I know some-one with a café there. Where would you want to live?"

Alistair looked as if I had just asked him the stupidest ques-tion that anyone could have asked him. He said, "How can you ask me such a stupid thing? You know we need to live in the States for your work. Even though the U.S. doesn't want us here, even though the U.S. treats its gay people like shit. Even though my countries, Australia or the U.K., actually respect gay people and would give us immigration rights. We need to be in the States because of you. I don't care where we live as long as we're together."

Oops. Having been called on my usual shit, I tried to buy some time by looking intelligent and tracing the outline of Madagascar with my left index finger. Don't try this, it never works. I've always loved maps. A lot of these maps here on my impressive set are maps I've had since I was a kid and got my first subscription to *National Geographic*. "Lands of the Bible." Here's a New York map from the day when I first set foot in Manhattan as a teenager. Staten Island didn't exist then. I loved board games with maps too. Candyland, the Game of Life, but I especially liked war games with maps. I guess it was one of the only places where my sissy self got to march to the approved martial parade: Stratego with its vaguely Napoleonic, Eurocentric map. Risk. What a fucked-up game! Risk taught generation after generation of young Americans how to fight the Cold War. How to mass your troops on the Soviet border for the final conflict. Monopoly—the sickest game ever created by late capitalism. What did Monopoly teach ten-year-olds but how to exploit the poor? How to charge as much rent as possible? I LOVED THESE GAMES! Some part of me, and not a small part either, believed that if I could learn how to play these games, if I could get blue or red Stratego pieces around the bombs, array my painted blue Risk squares cleverly along the border of the Ukraine, and most important, get the crucial two red hotels on Boardwalk and Park Place, then no one could fuck with me. I would never end up becoming a casualty of commerce or war. I think this is why I have often run my cavalry roughshod over the feelings of people I love. As I had just done, in fact, with my incredibly stupid question to Alistair the night before we were trying to get him back into the United States.

"I'm sorry, that was so stupid. I get freaked out too." I kissed his eyes as a way of apologizing.

"I get so scared," he whispered, turning his face away from the barrage of kisses. "What if it's like in ninety-seven when the U.S. wouldn't let me in? That almost destroyed us. Our whole life is in LA.. What would we do then?"

"I promise you, it'll be okay," I said, into Alistair's ear. "Why wouldn't they let you in? We're not doing anything wrong. We have the visa. We have the affidavit of support. I got a feeling this is gonna be fine. Trust me."

We kissed as we rolled over the map, our bodies crushing South America over Central Europe. South became East. North became West. The love and desire inside us melted these uncompromising boundaries. These noisy paper tectonics, courtesy of the National Geographic Society, crackled loud in our ears as we got ready to make love one more time, my hands on Alistair's skin. My hands charting his boundaries . . . My hands . . . my hands . . .

(Tim is caught in a follow spot as the stage goes dark and walks slowly into audience.)

My hands . . . my hands . . .
My hands have been slapped a lot in my life.

(Tim takes an audience member's hand in his and regards their palm.)

Most people think you learn about someone by reading the palm of the hand, but I think we can learn just as much from the back of our hands. You just need to be able to see the echo, the imprint of the times that that person's hand has been slapped.

My hand got slapped when I reached my hand into the cookie jar for just one more.

My hand got slapped when my first boyfriend was queer-bashed when I was eighteen. They yelled at him "Die Faggot Die" as they stabbed him nine times in the neck with an ice pick outside of a gay bar in Garden Grove, California.

My hand got slapped when certain right-wing congressmen said that no lesbian or gay artists should be able to raise their voices in America.

My hand got slapped very hard in fifth grade when I cut holes in the pockets of my pants. Neat Virgo holes here in my faggy maroon cords. I did this for a good reason, so I could put my fifth-grade fingers through those holes and touch my fifth-grade dick and balls during English lessons, subject-verb agreement. Now, this didn't hurt my command of the English language. I speak English very well. I have written a book. I'm a professor. My mom discovered my shame when she was hanging the washing up in the backyard to dry on the clothesline. She discovered the holes when she pulled the pockets inside out to dry better in the sun. She slapped my hands and said to me, "Don't fiddle! Don't fiddle! Don't fiddle!"

FIDDLE? I am always getting caught, caught red-handed.

(Tim heads back on stage, which floods with bright-as-noon Montana sunlight.)

We're here in Montana. Bozeman, Montana. It's 1997 Lesbian and Gay Pride Weekend in the state of Montana. BIG SKY PRIDE! I am here to perform for Montana Pride. Montana is a big state, about the size of western Europe, so people have to drive for twelve hours to get to Pride in Bozeman. There are about eight or nine hundred lesbians and gay men from around the state here. There are also about eight or nine hundred other people here to celebrate Gay Pride. The Montana militia has sent a bunch of folks. This was their fifteen minutes of fame what with the FBI stand-off that summer. The KKK has representatives from twelve counties in Wyoming, Montana, and Idaho. The White Aryan Nation has sent two busloads from Coeur d'Alene. We're all one big happy family here in America and we're all together to enjoy Montana Lesbian and Gay Pride. There are more pickup trucks with gun racks in the back than I have ever seen in my entire life. Unfortunately not one of them belongs to a butch dyke. I personally believe that lesbians are the only people who should be allowed to possess firearms in America. This is my version of gun control. It's been tense here, bomb threats, Montana State Police with telescopic rifles on the roofs of buildings on Main Street as we marched. This is one of those gigs I do in America, like in Chattanooga, where the police warn me for my safety to never stand in front of windows while the protesters wave their Confederate flags as the audience arrives for the show.

I am walking to a lesbian and gay wedding in Bozeman, Montana. I have done my performance the night before and now I'm going to take part in the last event of Pride weekend.

I am walking across a street in Bozeman on the way to the wedding and I can feel Alistair's hand in mine, his long cool fingers woven with mine. We've been through a lot in the last years. We're doing pretty good in 1997. We've gotten so much closer. Dealt with shit, I say "I love you" now without any rehearsal required. Everything is pretty good except for one thing. Alistair is not here with me. No Yellowstone vacation for us. Alistair is on the other side of the world being told by my government that he is not welcome here. He does not get to be in Montana holding the hand of his lover, boyfriend, husband, partner, I don't care what you call us. The U.S. consulate won't let him into the States, has rejected his student visa, his return ticket is no good now, and he has had to drop out of university because he's missed the beginning of the term and our lives are falling apart thanks to the U.S. government and I am walking across a street in Bozeman, Montana.

Two men in a pickup with a gun rack in the back window pull up and stop next to me. I know what's coming. I don't have to call the psychic friends network. What's coming is so predictable. What's coming are "F's."

Fucking.

Faggot.

Fruit.

Fairy.

Freak.

They're predictable, but they're scary too, like an angry dog straining at its leash. I know that those F's were usually followed by something more concrete—a rock, a bottle, maybe even a piece of concrete. Sure enough, a half-empty or, depending on your worldview, half-full bottle of Colt 45 Malt Liquor leaves the passenger-side window as it's flung at me. This was not an individual serving, this was a Sunday morning family-size bottle of Colt 45. It flew through the air, its geometry perfect. I could admire it for a moment even under these circumstances as it made a graceful arc and hit me direct on my right hand. My red, red hand—redder now from the hot blood dripping down my fingers. The bottle bounced and shattered at my feet. It's not too bad, five or six stitches tops, I just hope the guns stay in the gun rack.

I would like to say that at this moment I became homo superhero. I would tear off my clothes and instead of my vulnerable naked flesh, there would be an ugly superhero unitard costume. I would jump on the cab of their truck, kick the windshield in, and drag these two assholes across the broken glass. But I didn't do any of those things. I'm not strong enough, or dumb enough to do that. I wish I could be like my friend Mark in Iowa City. When someone yells "FAGGOT!" at him on the street, he has a commitment to immediately dropping his pants and underwear, turning his back to them, spreading his butt cheeks and shouting, "Yeah, I am a big faggot. Why don't you come here and lick my pussy!" I just can't do that. I guess I just don't have that spirit of Iowa in me. I just bowed my head and walked quicker, a deer frozen in the oncoming headlights. Well, the light changed and the men in the truck lost interest in me. They threw one or two more F's and then went on their way. I rubbed the blood, and the growing green and purple and red on my hand, my hand which just a moment before had been holding Alistair's. His hand slips into mine and the world goes mad. It's almost like they could see Alistair's hand in mine. It's not enough that our country has tried to destroy our relationship, these men in the truck still want to stick our hands in the frying pan, hold our hands to the flame as I cross a beautiful street in Montana made ugly by these men's hate.

Well, I wasn't much in the mood for going to a wedding now, but what else could I do? So off I went.

My hand aching for the absence of Alistair's hand in mine.

My head aching from the harsh ricochet of those F's.

My heart aching for these dozen lesbian and gay couples getting ready to bind their lives in an old school gymnasium in Bozeman, Montana.

(One last time Tim returns to Customs and Immigration. Uh oh.)

Alistair is next in line at Customs. He makes a shy smile and winks as he finally approaches the immigration officer and hands her his passport. She runs it through the scanner without even looking at him, and then looks through its pages.

"Business or pleasure, Mr. McCartney?"

"I'm a student," Al replies, shifting from foot to foot. "I'm here for study. I'm here to do an MFA in creative writing at Antioch University in Los Angeles."

The immigration officer suddenly looks down at her computer screen.

(Stage goes dark, leaving Tim in a follow spot. Two headlights pointed at the audience begin to glow.)

It's not a big look, but it's enough for me to know something bad is about to happen. She gestures to the armed immigration officer standing nearby, then looks directly at Alistair and says, "There's an irregularity in your request for a student visa. We have reason to believe that you have developed significant ties to an American citizen and that you will be a high risk for not leaving the U.S. at the end of your studies. Therefore, you are being denied entry to the U.S. and will be returned to Australia on the next plane. Please pick up your belongings and go along with this officer."

I can't breathe. I'm suddenly in a country that has no air for us. I tell myself I have to do whatever it takes to get one more breath. If I can just get one breath in, then another, then another.

Alistair says, "There must be a mistake in your records. I have a visa."

"There's no mistake, Mr. McCartney. Please go along with this officer."

I have no trouble breathing now. Great hyperventilating gasps rip into me. I drop my bag to the ground, cross the red line, and walk toward the immigration cop who is grabbing my boyfriend by the arm.

"Is there a problem here? Mr. McCartney is my . . . friend. I'm also his sponsor for his student visa."

"Please step back," the big cop says. "Now, sir."

"You don't understand, we're together."

Big Cop is getting angry. Pulling himself up he shouts, "Look, buddy, back off now or you're going to find yourself in big trouble."

I feel every moment I have been pushed around by cops, every time I have had a bottle thrown at me, every time I had felt my love for another man be shit on by my country.

I grab Alistair and pull him toward me. We hold each other very close. We're just having a bad dream. This isn't happening. We're still in Australia. We had too much Lebanese food the night before our trip and we're having a nightmare. We'll realize that it was just a crummy night's sleep and we'll start the day with a good cup of coffee and head off to the airport. But we do not wake up, and this is definitely not a dream.

"I love you, baby." I have no trouble saying the words now. "I love you too so much."

Wanting to impress his supervisor, Little Cop runs up and pulls us apart. He has a choke hold on Alistair and is dragging him away, pulling him toward a strange door covered in smoked glass. Big Cop has got me.

Alistair twists his face back over his shoulder as he is dragged toward the door. "Tim, do something! Don't let them send me back!" Alistair's shoulder bag is tugged down by Little Cop and spills open. His laptop clatters and breaks. There goes the novel. His notebook full of the love poems I sent him in London. A photo of us on vacation in Palm Springs. The intimacies of our life together are stripped naked, spread there on the concrete, exposed like film in the harsh light of this moment.

(The shock lights pointed at the audience begin to glow brighter and brighter.)

They are pulling Alistair into a room with opaque doors.

Big Cop drags me to the floor and pulls me toward the exit. "You assholes, he's my lover, my partner, my husband. You can't do this. I'm a fucking American citizen. I have rights! You can't do this."

The doors shut on Alistair. They have me down on the pavement and are dragging me away. The woman officer at her computer terminal regards this scene with annoyance. She glares at the U.S. citizens who have already made it through the lines, their mouths agape with the shame that comes when you watch injustice and do nothing. But all she says . . . "Next."

Next. Next. Next . . .

(The audience is blinded by the light. Tim picks very specific people and points at them with each "Next.")

I have one more thing in that hope chest. In that glory box. There's a compass inside.

(The shock lights fade on the audience. They're off the hook for now as a sweet quiet pulse of music comes up and one warm light illuminates Tim and the glory box.)

I hope that this compass will help me and Alistair avoid a future like that at some airport in America. But I have an even better compass inside me too. Right here in my hope chest. It's right where I knew it was. I was right when I was five. There is this place inside us. It's right here, behind my sternum and to the left of my heart. It's the compass that led me to love another man. It led me to love a man from another country. It led me around the world to find him. It led me up a stairway in London. Along a green river in Scotland. Across a street in New York. And by the sea in Venice Beach.

I want to use this compass to find my way to a place where Alistair and I can live. Where we can let our love grow deep. Where we can let our roots intertwine. Where we can learn, fight, grow, change, fuck up, make up, grow up just like other people.

I will use my compass to find a place where when two men kiss, the cop on the beat or the airplane captain in the cockpit will nod, smile, see us as the tin-canned newlyweds we are.

I want to use this compass to find my way to a place where our hands won't be pulled apart. Bed won't be torn in two. House won't be blown up. Bodies won't be flung to different hemispheres.

I want to use this compass to find my way to a place, to a field where two men or two women can come together and pledge their lives, their hopes, their fears, their failures, their myths, their memories, their bodies, and their goods in the sight of the gods, the goddesses, the state, the little children, and even my mom who I know will fly in special from Ventura, California. I don't want to have to leave my country to find this place. I don't want to be *forced* to leave my pathetic, frustrating, hate-filled, when-will-we-grow-up, annoying and ever beloved country. I may even want to use this compass to find that house with the ceramic elves. If I want to.

I'm going to use this compass to find my way home.

To find my way . . . to him.

(A very slow fade to black.)